The Magic of JELL-O®
BRAND

Above: Rainbow Ribbon Dessert

The Magic of JELL-O®
BRAND

100 New and Favorite Recipes
Celebrating 100 Years of Fun with JELL-O®

Sterling Publishing Co., Inc.
New York

Photography: Clive Champion, Chris Freeland, Robert Wigington
Food Stylists: Joan Ttooulias, Dennis Wood, Clare Stancer
Prop Stylist: Karen Martin
Recipe Editor: Mary Merlihan
French Version: Louise Boyer, Jocelyne Gingras
Cover/Inside Design & Art Direction:
Dave Hader/Studio Conceptions

Pictured on front cover:
Sparkling Fruits in Strawberry-Kiwi JELL-O®

Acknowledgements:

Among the many people who helped to produce this book, we would like to especially acknowledge Cécile Girard-Hicks, Director of the JELL-O Kitchens and her enthusiastic staff of food professionals including: Barb Martyn, Michele McAdoo, Maxine Karpel, Susanne Stark, Marian Macdonald, Marilynn Small, Judy Welden and Jane Carman.

Questions? Call the JELL-O Hotline. Your call will be answered by an experienced food professional—one of the helpful staff in the JELL-O Kitchens.

The JELL-O Hotline is open Monday to Friday 9:00 a.m. until 4:00 p.m. (E.S.T.). Any questions or comments, please feel free to call 1-800-431-1001.

10 9 8 7 6 5 4 3 2 1

Published in 2001 by Sterling Publishing Co., Inc.
387 Park Avenue South, New York, NY 10016

First published in Canada by MGR Publishing & Promotions Inc., Toronto

Manufactured in China

ISBN 0-8069-7703-5

The Magic of JELL-O® BRAND

Dear JELL-O Consumer,

We invite you to celebrate this historical JELL-O moment with us.

A great team has worked very hard to put this book together for you. From left to right: Susanne Stark, Cécile Girard-Hicks, Michele McAdoo, Barb Martyn.

JELL-O Brand is now 101 years old - we like to think of it as 101 years young — so we've gathered 100 of the top-rated JELL-O ideas of all time and put them in this memorial cookbook to you.

We can't think of another food that has been so popular for so many years - to so many people of all ages. Nothing feels like JELL-O in your mouth, dances like JELL-O on your plate. Nothing can go from simple to sophisticated so easily.

This cookbook will take you from the JELL-O classics you enjoyed growing up to the latest up-to-the-minute products and recipes. Everything from our ready-to-eat line of gelatin and pudding snacks to simple, sensational recipes for things like Trifle and Cappuccino Cups.

There's a section for novices and experts alike; a special section for kids; another one for the health-conscious called Light Delights. (It's reassuring to know that JELL-O Gelatin Dessert is fat free and very low in calories.)

Everything in this book has been tested in our own kitchens to make sure it's as easy as it can be and because we know how much you like to see what you're making, we have a photograph with each recipe.

The magic of JELL-O is all here for you to rediscover and we hope you have as much pleasure making these recipes as we did putting them together.

From the food experts of the Kraft Kitchens

CONTENTS

TRICKS OF THE TRADE

For best results when preparing JELL-O Gelatin Dessert according to package directions, follow these easy guidelines.

1. To make a mixture that is clear and uniformly set, be sure the gelatin is completely dissolved in boiling water or other boiling liquid before adding the cold liquid. Stirring with a rubber spatula will help ensure that all the crystals are dissolved.

2. To store prepared gelatin overnight or longer, cover it to prevent drying.

3. To speed up chilling time, choose the right container. A metal bowl or mold will chill the gelatin faster than glass. Individual servings in small molds or serving dishes will chill more quickly than large servings.

4. The 30 Minute Set Method is a quick way to set gelatin. Refer to directions on the package. Do not use this method for molding gelatin.

5. Do not use fresh or frozen pineapple, kiwi, gingerroot, papaya, figs or guava. Gelatin will not set properly.

6. For skinless cooked pudding, cool for 10 minutes after cooking, stir and place plastic wrap directly on surface of pudding. Chill for 30 minutes then stir and fill serving dishes. Serve warm or cold. By the way, warm pudding is extra delicious.

7. Try making gelatin in the blender. Empty 1 pkg (85 g) JELL-O Gelatin Dessert into blender. Add 1 cup (250 mL) boiling water. Blend on low speed to dissolve gelatin, about 30 seconds. Add 2 cups (500 mL) ice cubes. Blend at high speed until ice is melted. Chill in individual glasses 20 minutes. This forms a two layered dessert as it sets.

GELATIN CHILLING TIME CHART

Use this chart as a guildine to determine the desired consistency and the approximate chilling time.

WHEN RECIPE SAYS:	IT MEANS GELATIN SHOULD ...	SET TIME FOR REGULAR METHOD	SET TIME FOR 30 MINUTE SET METHOD	USE IT FOR
"Chill until slightly thickened"	Gelatin should be consistency of unbeaten egg whites	1¼ hours	3 to 5 minutes	Adding creamy ingredients such as whipped topping, or when mixture will be beaten
"Chill until set but not firm"	Stick to the finger when touched and should mound or move to the side when bowl or mold is tilted	2 hours	30 minutes	Layering gelatin mixture i.e. molds
"Chill until firm"	Not stick to finger when touched and not mound or move when mold is tilted.	Individual molds at least 3 hours 2 to 6 cup molds at least 4 hours 8 to 12 cup molds at least 5 hours or overnight		Unmolding and serving

THE SECRET TO MOLDING GELATIN

THE MOLD

Use metal, plastic, square or round cake pans, fluted or plain tube pans, loaf pans, metal mixing bowls.

To determine the volume of the mold, measure first with water. Most recipes give an indication of the size of the mold needed.

For easier unmolding, spray the mold with nonstick cooking spray before filling with gelatin or brush lightly with vegetable oil.

Use less water in preparing gelatin for molding. For a 4-serving size package, reduce the cold water by ¼ cup (50 mL). The adjustment has already been made in recipes in this book.

To arrange fruits or vegetables in molds, chill gelatin until slightly thickened. Pour gelatin into mold to about ¼-inch (.5 cm) depth. Arrange fruits or vegetables in decorative pattern in gelatin. Chill until set but not firm, then pour remaining thickened gelatin over pattern in mold.

To prevent spilling, place mold on tray in refrigerator before pouring in gelatin.

TO UNMOLD, always allow gelatin to set until firm by refrigerating several hours or overnight.

Moisten tips of fingers and gently pull gelatin from around edge of mold. Or, use a small metal spatula or pointed knife dipped in warm water to loosen top edge.

Dip mold in warm, not hot, water, just to rim, for about 15 seconds. Lift from water, hold upright and shake to loosen gelatin. Or, gently pull gelatin from edge of mold.

Moisten chilled serving plate with water. (This allows gelatin to be moved after unmolding.) Place moistened serving plate on top of mold. Invert mold and plate; holding mold and plate together, shake slightly to loosen. Gently remove mold. If gelatin does not release easily, dip mold in warm water again for a few seconds. Center gelatin on serving plate.

OTHER PREPARATION TRICKS

Always dissolve Gelatin Dessert in boiling water, stirring for 2 minutes to be sure to dissolve all crystals. A rubber spatula works well to dissolve crystals.

For 30 Minute Set Method, dissolve 1 pkg (85g) JELL-O Gelatin Dessert in 1 cup (250 mL) boiling water. Add 2 cups (500 mL) ice cubes. Stir until gelatin thickens, about 3 to 5 minutes. Remove only unmelted ice. Chill 30 minutes.

To flake gelatin, prepare gelatin as directed on package, reducing cold water to ¾ cup (175 mL). Pour into a shallow pan and chill until firm, about 2 hours. To flake, break gelatin into small flakes with a fork and pile lightly into dishes, alone or with fruit or whipped topping.

To prepare gelatin cubes, prepare gelatin as above for flaking. Cut gelatin into small cubes, using a sharp knife that has been dipped in hot water. To remove cubes from pan, quickly dip pan in warm water and remove with lifter. Serve in dishes with whipped topping or fruit, if desired.

To fold whipped topping into partially set gelatin, use a rubber spatula and fold using an over and under motion, being careful not to 'mix' but to 'fold'. For a smooth mixture, be sure gelatin is partially set, not too firm or your mixture will be lumpy.

To whip gelatin, prepare gelatin as directed on package. Chill until slightly thickened. Beat on high speed of electric mixer until light and fluffy, about 3 minutes. Or use 30 Minute Set Method, to 'slightly thickened' and beat as above.

JELL-O

Fun for Kids

Busy Bees

Prep time: 15 minutes   Chill time: 1 hour

1 pkg	(4-serving size) JELL-O Grape Gelatin Dessert	**1 pkg**
1 pkg	(4-serving size) JELL-O Vanilla Instant Pudding & Pie Filling	**1 pkg**
10	Chocolate wafer cookies	**10**
	Black shoestring licorice	

▼ **PREPARE** Gelatin Dessert according to package directions, reducing cold water to ½ cup (125 mL); pour into shallow pan and chill until set, about 1 hr.

▼ **PREPARE** pudding according to package directions, reducing milk to 1½ cups (375 mL); chill 5 minutes.

▼ **TO MAKE** bees, break gelatin into small pieces using fork. Alternately layer gelatin and pudding in small plastic or glass cups, ending with pudding layer.

▼ **GARNISH** each bee with two chocolate wafer cookies for "wings", 1 black jelly candy for a "head" and 2 pieces of black shoestring licorice for "antennae".

MAKES 5 bees.

TIP: *For easy blending, use a wire whisk to blend pudding and milk.*

Berry Blue Shooting Stars

Prep time: 10 minutes   Chill time: 30 minutes

1 cup	boiling water	**250 mL**
1 pkg	(4-serving size) JELL-O Berry Blue Gelatin Dessert	**1 pkg**
2 cups	ice cubes	**500 mL**
1 cup	thawed COOL WHIP Whipped Topping	**250 mL**
	Additional thawed COOL WHIP Whipped Topping	
4	marshmallows	**4**
	Colored sugar	

▼ **ADD** boiling water to Gelatin Dessert. Stir until completely dissolved. Add ice cubes. Stir until gelatin thickens (3 to 5 minutes). Remove any unmelted ice.

▼ **SPOON** thickened gelatin into dessert dishes alternately with spoonfuls of whipped topping to form clouds. Refrigerate until set, about 30 minutes.

▼ **GARNISH** with additional whipped topping and marshmallows, cut into star shapes and sprinkled with colored sugar.

MAKES 4 servings.

TIP: *To cut marshmallows, flatten slightly with rolling pin and cut with star cutter. Moisten slightly with water and sprinkle with colored sugar.*

SLUSHIES

Prep time: 5 minutes   Freezing time: 4 hours or overnight

1 pkg	(4-serving size) JELL-O Gelatin Dessert, any flavor	**1 pkg**
1 cup	boiling water	**250 mL**
2 cups	ginger ale	**500 mL**

- ▼ **DISSOLVE** Gelatin Dessert in boiling water.
- ▼ **ADD** ginger ale and pour into an 8 inch (20 cm) square pan. Freeze until firm, 4 hours or overnight
- ▼ **TO SERVE**, use an ice cream scoop to fill serving dishes, paper cups or ice cream cones. Serve immediately.

MAKES 4 servings.

TIP: *Substitute your favorite carbonated beverage for the ginger ale. Serve with sliced fresh fruit, if desired.*

BLOOMING BERRY FLOWERS

Prep time: 15 minutes Chill time: 3 hours

2 pkg	(4-serving size) JELL-O Strawberry Gelatin Dessert, or your favorite flavor	**2 pkg**
1¼ cups	boiling water	**300 mL**
4	paper cups (5 oz/147.8 mL each)	**4**
Flowers	Large marshmallows, colored sprinkles, colored coconut, candies, toothpicks, plastic straws cut in half.	

▼ **DISSOLVE** Gelatin Dessert in boiling water, stirring until completely dissolved, about 2 minutes. Pour into paper cups.

▼ **REFRIGERATE** until firm, at least 3 hours.

▼ **CUT** marshmallows into five pieces using scissors to make flower petals. Arrange petals in flower shape, pressing each petal tightly together. Press colored sprinkles or coconut onto petals and candy for center.

▼ **INSERT** toothpick through center of marshmallow flowers. Place toothpick into straw.

▼ **CAREFULLY** peel away paper cups from gelatin. Place on serving plate and insert flower straw in center of pot.

MAKES 4 flower pots.

TIP: *Be sure to press marshmallows together when freshly cut and still sticky, so they hold together well.*

CHOCOLATE PUDDING CATS

Prep time: 10 minutes

1 pkg	(4-serving size) JELL-O Chocolate Instant Pudding & Pie Filling	**1 pkg**
2 cups	milk	**500 mL**
	Assorted candies: shoestring and assorted licorice, jelly beans, jujubes, etc.	

▼ **PREPARE** pudding according to package directions. Spoon into 4 round bowls. Let stand 5 minutes.

▼ **DECORATE** with candies to resemble cat faces.

MAKES 4 servings.

TIP: *Use an assortment of fruit slices instead of candy to make face, i.e. banana slices, strawberry slices, mandarin oranges.*

COOKIE DUNK PUDDING

Prep time: 10 minutes

2 cups	cold milk	**500 mL**
1 pkg	(4-serving size) JELL-O Instant Pudding & Pie Filling, any flavor	**1 pkg**
20-30	miniature cookies	**20-30**

▼ **POUR** milk into medium bowl. Add pudding mix. Beat at low speed with electric mixer or with wire whisk until well blended, 1 to 2 minutes. Let stand 5 minutes.

▼ **SPOON** half of the pudding into 4 dessert dishes. Stand 4 to 6 cookies in each dish of pudding, placing them along sides of dish. Top with remaining pudding.

▼ **SERVE** immediately or refrigerate until ready to serve. Garnish with a dollop of whipped topping and additional cookies, if desired.

MAKES 4 servings.

TIP: *If desired, break larger cookies into 4 pieces and substitute for the miniature cookies.*

DIRT CUPS

Prep time: 10 minutes

1 pkg	(4-serving size) JELL-O Chocolate Instant Pudding & Pie Filling	**1 pkg**
2 cups	thawed COOL WHIP Whipped Topping	**500 mL**
20	chocolate sandwich cookies, crushed (“dirt”)	**20**
	Gummy worms	

▼ **PREPARE** pudding according to package directions.

▼ **FOLD** in whipped topping and half of crushed cookies.

▼ **TO ASSEMBLE,** place about 1 Tbsp (15 mL) crushed cookies in bottom of 6 dessert dishes. Fill dishes three-quarter full with pudding mixture. Top with remaining crushed cookies. Garnish with gummy worms.

▼ **CHILL** if not serving immediately.

MAKES 6 servings.

TIP: *A fun idea for a kids party. Make in paper cups.*

ALASKAN PUDDING PIES

Prep time: 10 minutes   Freezing time: 3 hours

1 cup	cold milk	**250 mL**
1 pkg	(4-serving size) JELL-O Chocolate Instant Pudding & Pie Filling, or your favorite flavor	**1 pkg**
2 cups	thawed COOL WHIP Whipped Topping	**500 mL**
36	large cookies, your favorite variety (chocolate chip, double chocolate)	**36**

▼ **COMBINE** milk and pudding mix; blend well. Fold into topping.

▼ **SPREAD** filling about ½-inch (1 cm) thick on half of the cookies. Top with remaining cookies, pressing lightly and smoothing around edges with knife.

▼ **FREEZE** until firm, about 3 hours. Store in covered container in freezer or wrap individually and store in freezer.

MAKES 18 snacks.

TIP: *Add ½ cup (125 mL) chocolate chips or nuts to pudding mixture. Roll "pies" in chocolate chips or colored sprinkles before freezing, if desired.*

FRUITY PIZZA FAVORITES

Prep time: 15 minutes Chill time: 3 hours or overnight

2 pkg	(4-serving size) JELL-O Grape Gelatin Dessert	**2 pkg**
2 cups	boiling water	**500 mL**
1 cup	cold water	**250 mL**
	Thawed COOL WHIP Whipped Topping	
	Assortment of fresh fruit pieces for decoration	

▼ **DISSOLVE** Gelatin Dessert in boiling water, stirring until completely dissolved, about 2 minutes. Stir in cold water. Pour into 13 x 9 inch (33 x 23 cm) pan.

▼ **REFRIGERATE** until firm, 3 hours or overnight.

▼ **TO ASSEMBLE**, place about 4 inches (10 cm) of warm, **not hot**, water in sink. Dip pan in water just to top of pan for 5 seconds. Cut out circles using a 4 inch (10 cm) round cookie cutter or rim of a drinking glass. Lift carefully out of pan and place on serving plate.

▼ **SPOON** whipped topping onto center of gelatin, and spread to within ½-inch (1 cm) of edge.

▼ **DECORATE** with pieces of fruit.

MAKES 6 pizzas.

TIP: *Use leftover gelatin layered in dessert dishes, with whipped topping and fruit.*

JELL-O® JIGGLERS®

Prep time: 3 minutes   Chill time: 3 hours

2 pkg	(8-serving size) JELL-O Gelatin Dessert, any flavor	**2 pkg**
	OR	
4 pkg	(4-serving size) JELL-O Gelatin Dessert, any flavor	**4 pkg**
2½ cups	boiling water or boiling juice	**625 mL**

▼ **DISSOLVE** Gelatin Dessert in boiling water or boiling juice. Pour into 13 x 9 inch (33 x 23 cm) pan. Chill for 3 hours or until firm.

▼ **TO UNMOLD**, dip pan in warm water about 15 seconds. Cut into squares or use cookie cutters. Lift from pan. Store in refrigerator until needed.

MAKES about 24 jigglers.

TIP: *For easy dissolving of Gelatin Dessert, use a rubber spatula to stir and dissolve. This should take about 3 minutes.*

JELL-O® MILK JIGGLERS®

Prep time: 5 minutes   Chill time: 3 hours

4 pkg	(4-serving size) JELL-O Gelatin Dessert, your favorite flavor	**4 pkg**
1 cup	boiling water	**250 mL**
1½ cups	milk	**375 mL**

▼ **DISSOLVE** Gelatin Dessert in boiling water. Cool to room temperature. Gradually stir in milk.

▼ **POUR** into 13 x 9 inch (33 x 23 cm) pan.

▼ **CHILL** for 3 hours or until firm.

▼ **TO UNMOLD**, dip pan in warm water about 15 seconds. Cut into squares or use cookie cutters. Lift from pan. Store in refrigerator until needed.

MAKES about 24 jigglers.

TIP: *For easy dissolving of Gelatin Dessert, use a rubber spatula to stir and dissolve. This should take about 3 minutes. Be sure to cool gelatin down before adding milk or it will curdle.*

LOLLIPOP JIGGLES

Prep time: 10 minutes Chill time: 3 hours

1¼ cups	boiling water	**300 mL**
2 pkg	(4-serving size) JELL-O Gelatin Dessert, any flavor	**2 pkg**
4	small paper cups	**4**
6	plastic straws, cut in half	**6**

▼ **ADD** boiling water to Gelatin Dessert. Stir until completely dissolved. Let stand to cool for 15 minutes.

▼ **POUR** into paper cups. Refrigerate until firm at least 3 hours.

▼ **CAREFULLY** peel away cups. Using a knife dipped in warm water, cut each gelatin cup horizontally into 3 round slices.

▼ **INSERT** straw half into each gelatin slice to resemble a lollipop.

MAKES 12 pops.

TIP: *Substitue ½ cup (125 mL) boiling fruit juice for ½ cup (125 mL) boiling water, if desired.*

Pudding Fun Pops

Prep time: 5 minutes   Freezing time: 4 hours or overnight

3 cups	milk	**750 mL**
1 pkg	(4-serving size) JELL-O Instant Pudding & Pie Filling, any flavor	**1 pkg**
9	(3 oz / 85 mL) small paper cups	**9**
9	popsicle sticks	**9**

▼ **POUR** milk into a bowl. Add pudding to milk and beat with wire whisk until smooth, about 2 minutes.

▼ **SET** paper cups on cookie sheet. Pour pudding mixture into paper cups. Insert a popsicle stick into center of each cup.

▼ **FREEZE** until firm, about 4 hours or overnight. If not using pops within 24 hours, store in a plastic bag. Dip pops in hot water for 10 seconds to unmold.

MAKES 9 pops.

VARIATION:

Make a S'More Pop! Place 3 or 4 miniature marshmallows and 1 tsp (5 mL) BAKER'S Miniature Chocolate Chips in bottom of each cup before filling with pudding.

TIP: *Use your favorite popsicle molds instead of the cups.*

ICY BLUE IGLOO

Prep time: 20 minutes   Chill time: 3 hours

3 pkg	(4-serving size) JELL-O Berry Blue Gelatin Dessert	**3 pkg**
2¾ cups	boiling water	**675 mL**
1½ cups	cold water	**375 mL**
2 cups	ice cubes	**500 mL**
2 cups	thawed COOL WHIP Whipped Topping	**500 mL**

▼ **DISSOLVE** 2 packages of Gelatin Dessert in 2 cups (500 mL) boiling water. Add cold water. Pour into 13 x 9 inch (33 x 23 cm) pan. Chill until set, about 3 hours. Cut gelatin into ½ inch (1 cm) cubes. Set aside.

▼ **LINE** a 6 cup (1.5 L) bowl with plastic wrap. Set aside.

▼ **DISSOLVE** remaining package of Gelatin Dessert in ¾ cup (175 mL) boiling water. Add ice cubes. Stir until slightly thickened, about 3 to 5 minutes. Remove any unmelted ice. Whisk in 1 cup (250 mL) whipped topping. Stir in ⅔ of the gelatin cubes and pour mixture into prepared bowl. Chill until set, about 3 hours.

▼ **UNMOLD** onto serving plate. Remove plastic wrap and frost surface with remaining whipped topping and decorate with remaining gelatin cubes.

MAKES 8 servings.

TIP: *To make 4 individual igloos, divide gelatin mixture between 4 small bowls lined with plastic wrap and continue as directed above. The kids can have some fun and frost and decorate their own igloo.*

SQUISHAROOS

Prep time: 5 minutes

1 pkg	(4-serving size) JELL-O Gelatin Dessert, any flavor	**1 pkg**
24	large marshmallows	**24**

▼ **EMPTY** Gelatin Dessert into a large plastic bag.

▼ **MOISTEN** marshmallows with water and shake 3 or 4 at a time in Gelatin Dessert to coat.

MAKES about two dozen.

***TIP**: If desired, cut marshmallows into fun shapes by flattening slightly and cutting with small cutters.*

SUPER NO-DRIP POPS

Prep time: 5 minutes   Freezing time: 3 hours or overnight

1 pkg	(4-serving size) JELL-O Gelatin Dessert, any flavor	**1 pkg**
1 pouch	(135 g) KOOL-AID Sugar-Sweetened Drink Mix, any flavor	**1 pouch**
2 cups	boiling water	**500 mL**
1½ cups	cold water	**375 mL**
11	(3 oz/85 mL) paper cups	**11**
11	popsicle sticks	**11**

- ▼ **DISSOLVE** Gelatin Dessert and drink mix in boiling water. Add cold water.
- ▼ **SET** paper cups on cookie sheet. Pour gelatin mixture into paper cups.
- ▼ **FREEZE** until partially set, about 2 hours.
- ▼ **INSERT** a popsicle stick into center of each cup. Freeze until firm.

MAKES about 11 pops.

TIPS: *Use your own popsicle containers, if desired.*

Substitute fruit juice for the cold water, if desired.

Treasure Chests

Prep time: 15 minutes   Chill time: 3 hours or overnight

2 pkg	(4-serving size) JELL-O Grape Gelatin Dessert	**2 pkg**
2 cups	boiling water	**500 mL**
1 cup	cold water	**250 mL**
	Thawed COOL WHIP Whipped Topping	
	Candies, Chocolate Wafers for decorations	

- **DISSOLVE** Gelatin Dessert in boiling water, stirring until completely dissolved, about 2 minutes. Stir in cold water. Pour into 8 x 4 inch (20 x 12 cm) loaf pan.
- **REFRIGERATE** until firm, 3 hours or overnight.
- **DIP** cake pan in warm water just to top of pan for 5 seconds. Unmold onto board.
- **DIVIDE** gelatin into 4 equal treasure chests. Cut a small section from center of each chest, leaving a 1 inch (2.5 cm) border.
- **FILL** cavity with whipped topping and candies. Use 2 chocolate wafers for lid of each treasure chest.

MAKES 4 treasure chests.

***TIP:** Use fruit pieces instead of candies, if desired.*

WATERMELON PIT PARFAIT

Prep time: 10 minutes   Chill time: 30 minutes

2 cups	thawed COOL WHIP Whipped Topping	**500 mL**
5 drops	green food coloring	**5 drops**
1 cup	boiling water	**250 mL**
1 pkg	(4-serving size) JELL-O Watermelon Gelatin Dessert	**1 pkg**
2 cups	ice cubes	**500 mL**
2 Tbsp	BAKER'S Miniature Semi-Sweet Chocolate Chips	**25 mL**

▼ **MIX** whipped topping with food coloring. Spread green topping evenly inside 4 dessert dishes to make "rind". Place in freezer while preparing gelatin.

▼ **ADD** boiling water to Gelatin Dessert. Stir until completely dissolved. Add ice cubes. Stir until slightly thickened, 3 to 5 minutes. Remove any unmelted ice. Spoon into prepared dessert dishes.

▼ **POKE** chocolate chips into gelatin to make "seeds". Chill 30 minutes.

MAKES 4 desserts.

TIP: *For best results, use a rubber spatula when dissolving Gelatin Dessert in boiling water.*

WIGGLY BANANA SPLITS

Prep time: 15 minutes   Chill time: 3 hours

1 pkg	(4-serving size) JELL-O Watermelon or Strawberry-Kiwi Gelatin Dessert	**1 pkg**
1 cup	boiling water	**250 mL**
¾ cup	cold water	**175 mL**
1 pkg	(4-serving size) JELL-O Vanilla Instant Pudding & Pie Filling	**1 pkg**
4	small bananas, peeled and sliced lengthwise	**4**
1 cup	thawed COOL WHIP Whipped Topping	**250 mL**
4	maraschino cherries	**4**

- **DISSOLVE** Gelatin Dessert in boiling water. Add cold water. Pour into an 8 inch (20 cm) square pan. Refrigerate until firm, about 3 hours.
- **PREPARE** pudding as directed on package.
- **CUT** gelatin into small cubes. Place a few cubes on bottom of each dish. Top with some of the pudding.
- **TOP** with sliced bananas, more pudding, cubes, whipped topping and cherries.

MAKES 4 servings.

TIP: *Dip bananas in lemon juice to prevent browning.*

WIGGLY WATERMELON WORMS

Prep time: 10 minutes   Chill time: 45 minutes

1 pkg	(4-serving size) JELL-O Watermelon Gelatin Dessert	**1 pkg**
½ cup	warm water	**125 mL**
1½ cups	miniature marshmallows	**375 mL**
4	chocolate wafer cookies, crushed ("dirt", optional)	**4**
	Black shoestring licorice	

▼ **SPRAY** a 8 or 9 inch (20 or 23 cm) square pan with a non-stick cooking spray. Spread on bottom and sides of pan with paper towel.

▼ **MIX** Gelatin Dessert and warm water in medium microwavable bowl.

▼ **MICROWAVE** on HIGH 1½ minutes. Stir to dissolve completely.

▼ **ADD** marshmallows and microwave on HIGH 1 minute or until marshmallows are puffed and almost melted. Stir mixture slowly until marshmallows are completely melted and mixture is smooth. (Creamy layer will float to top.)

▼ **POUR** into prepared pan. Refrigerate 45 minutes or until set. Loosen edges with knife. Cut into 16, ½ inch (1 cm) strips.

▼ **SNIP** licorice into small pieces for eyes and attach to "worms."

▼ **SPRINKLE** cookie crumbs on a plate to resemble dirt. Place "Worms" on top of dirt.

MAKES 16 pieces.

TIP: *These "worms" can be made with any flavor of JELL-O. They may also be made in a saucepan on top of the stove. Combine Gelatin Dessert and warm water in a saucepan over medium heat. Stir to dissolve, about 2 minutes, stir in marshmallows and heat until melted, about 2 minutes. Remove and proceed as above.*

Razzle Dazzle Berry Mousse

Prep time: 10 minutes   Chill time: 10 minutes

1 pkg	(4-serving size) JELL-O Strawberry Gelatin Dessert	**1 pkg**
1 cup	boiling water	**250 mL**
1 pkg	(300 g) frozen unsweetened strawberries	**1 pkg**
1½ cups	thawed COOL WHIP Whipped Topping	**375 mL**

▼ **DISSOLVE** Gelatin Dessert in boiling water. Add frozen strawberries, breaking apart with a fork. Stir until slightly thickened, 3 to 5 minutes.

▼ **FOLD** in whipped topping. Pour into dessert dishes. Chill 10 minutes.

MAKES 6 servings.

TIP: *For Raspberry Mousse, use 1 pkg (85 g) JELL-O Raspberry Gelatin Dessert and 1 pkg (300 g) frozen unsweetened raspberries.*

Citrus Meringue

Prep time: 10 minutes   Chill time: 10 minutes

1 pkg	(4-serving size) JELL-O Lemon Gelatin Dessert	**1 pkg**
1½ cups	peeled and chopped orange and grapefruit segments	**375 mL**

▼ **PREPARE** Gelatin Dessert according to 30 Minute Set Method on package.

▼ **SET ASIDE** ⅔ cup (150 mL) of slightly thickened gelatin. Stir fruit into remaining gelatin; spoon into 4 dessert dishes.

▼ **BEAT** reserved gelatin with electric mixer until double in volume. Spoon over fruited layer in dishes. Chill until set, about 10 minutes.

MAKES 4 servings.

TIP: *For best results when beating gelatin - it must be of egg white consistency before beating.*

DID YOU KNOW HOW TO PEEL AND SEGMENT CITRUS FRUITS:

Cut off both ends of fruit. Cut the skin working down the rounded slope of the fruit, cutting off both pith and peel. Hold peeled fruit and slice down between membranes to free each segment.

CREAMY MOUSSE DELIGHT

Prep time: 10 minutes   Chill time: 30 minutes

1 pkg	(4-serving size) JELL-O Instant Pudding & Pie Filling, any flavor	**1 pkg**
2 cups	thawed COOL WHIP or COOL WHIP LITE Whipped Topping	**500 mL**

- **PREPARE** pudding as directed on package.
- **FOLD** in whipped topping.
- **SPOON** into individual dessert dishes. Chill about 30 minutes.

MAKES 6 servings.

TIP: *Fold in 1 (40 to 50 g) chopped chocolate bar of your choice.*

FRUITY SHAKES

Prep time: 10 minutes

½ cup	boiling water	**125 mL**
1 pkg	(4-serving size) JELL-O Berry Blue Gelatin Dessert	**1 pkg**
2 cups	vanilla ice cream	**500 mL**
1 cup	milk	**250 mL**
½ cup	crushed ice	**125 mL**

- **POUR** water in electric blender container. Add Gelatin Dessert. Cover and blend at medium speed for 1 minute. Scrape sides of container.
- **WITH** machine running, add ice cream by spoonfuls through hole in lid of blender.
- **ADD** milk and ice; blend at medium speed for 30 seconds. Serve immediately.

MAKES 3 to 4 servings.

TIP: *Use any flavor of Gelatin Dessert and add ½ cup (125 mL) fruit to the blender with the ice cream, if desired.*

DID YOU KNOW ABOUT FROZEN FRUIT:

For maximum freshness, use in 3 months. Do not hold longer than 6 months. Do not refreeze thawed fruit. To thaw fruit, place unopened package in bowl. Allow to stand at room temperature for 2½ hours.

Opposite page: Citrus Meringue, Razzle Dazzle Berry Mousse, Creamy Mousse Delight

Above: Fruity Shakes

Quick and Easy Butterscotch Fudge

Prep time: 10 minutes   Chill time: 1 hour

¼ cup	milk	**50 mL**
1 pkg	(6-serving size) JELL-O Butterscotch Pudding & Pie Filling	**1 pkg**
3 Tbsp	butter	**45 mL**
2¼ cups	sifted powdered sugar	**525 mL**
⅔ cup	chopped nuts	**150 mL**

- ▼ **LINE** a small loaf pan with waxed paper.
- ▼ **BLEND** milk gradually into pudding mix in a medium microwavable bowl. Add butter.
- ▼ **COOK** uncovered on HIGH power for 1 minute. Stir well. Cook on HIGH power for 1 minute. Mixture should just start to foam or boil around the edges. Do not overcook. Stir well.
- ▼ **QUICKLY** blend in powdered sugar and nuts.
- ▼ **POUR** into pan and chill 45 minutes to one hour. Cut into pieces. Store in refrigerator.

MAKES 18 to 24 pieces.

NOTE: Tested in 700 watt oven. For 500 watt oven increase second cooking time to 65 seconds.

TIP: *Use JELL-O Chocolate or Vanilla Pudding and Pie Filling, if desired. Add ½ cup (125 mL) dried fruit such as apricots, cranberries or candied cherries, if desired.*

Above: Quick and Easy Butterscotch Fudge

Creamy Delight Cups

Prep time: 15 minutes Chill time: 30 minutes

1 pkg	(4-serving size) JELL-O Gelatin Dessert, any flavor	**1 pkg**
1 cup	boiling water	**250 mL**
2 cups	vanilla ice cream	**500 mL**

▼ **DISSOLVE** Gelatin Dessert in boiling water. Cool in refrigerator for about 10 minutes.

▼ **WHISK** in ice cream.

▼ **POUR** into individual dessert dishes, chill until set, about 30 minutes.

MAKES 6 servings.

TIP: *Adding ice cream makes this recipe set in 30 minutes. Be creative with your favorite ice cream and JELL-O flavors. Substitute frozen yogurt for ice cream, if desired.*

Quick and Easy Fluffy Mousse

Prep time: 15 minutes Chill time: 1 hour

1 pkg	(4-serving size) JELL-O Gelatin Dessert, any flavor	**1 pkg**
2 cups	thawed COOL WHIP or COOL WHIP LITE Whipped Topping	**500 mL**

▼ **PREPARE** Gelatin Dessert according to 30 Minute Set Method on package.

▼ **REMOVE** any unmelted ice cubes, fold in whipped topping.

▼ **CHILL** until set, about 1 hour.

MAKES 6 servings.

TIP: *Add ½ cup (125 mL) sliced fruit after removing ice cubes, if desired.*

Juicy JELL-O® Cups

Prep time: 10 minutes Chill time: 1 hour

1 pkg	(4-serving size) JELL-O Gelatin Dessert, any flavor	**1 pkg**
1 cup	fruit juice	**250 mL**

▼ **PREPARE** Gelatin Dessert with 1 cup (250 mL) boiling water. Stir in fruit juice in place of cold water.

▼ **CHILL** in individual dessert dishes until set, about 1 hour.

MAKES 4 servings.

TIP: *Use JELL-O Strawberry Gelatin Dessert and apple juice or JELL-O Cranberry Gelatin Dessert with orange or raspberry juice or experiment with your own flavor combo.*

IT'S SO QUICK AND EASY WITH JELL-O®

By simply adding thawed COOL WHIP Whipped Topping, fruit juice, carbonated beverages, ice cream, milk and yogurt to JELL-O Gelatin Dessert you can create fun desserts that your whole family will love. See pages 38 and 40.

Above: Quick and Easy JELL-O® Desserts

JELL-O® SMOOTHY

Prep time: 15 minutes   Chill time: 30 minutes

1 pkg	(4-serving size) JELL-O Gelatin Dessert, any flavor	**1 pkg**
1 cup	boiling water	**250 mL**
2 cups	plain or fruit yogurt or frozen vanilla yogurt	**500 mL**

▼ **DISSOLVE** Gelatin Dessert in boiling water. Cool in refrigerator for about 10 minutes .

▼ **WHISK** in yogurt.

▼ **PLACE** in refrigerator and chill until set, about 30 minutes.

Makes 4 servings.

***TIP:** Make sure water has just boiled for best dissolving of Gelatin Dessert.*

JELL-O® COW

Prep time: 15 minutes   Chill time: 1 hour

1 pkg	(4-serving size) JELL-O Gelatin Dessert, any flavor	**1 pkg**
1 cup	boiling water	**250 mL**
2 cups	milk	**500 mL**

▼ **DISSOLVE** Gelatin Dessert in boiling water. Cool to room temperature.

▼ **GRADUALLY** stir in milk. Pour into dessert dishes.

▼ **CHILL** until set, about 1 hour.

MAKES 6 servings.

***TIP:** Cooling the gelatin is very important or the milk will curdle.*

JELL-O® REFRESHERS

Prep time: 5 minutes   Chill time: 3 hours

1 pkg	(4-serving size) JELL-O Gelatin Dessert, any flavor	**1 pkg**
1 cup	boiling water	**250 mL**
1 cup	cold carbonated beverage	**250 mL**

▼ **DISSOLVE** Gelatin Dessert in boiling water. Cool to room temperature.

▼ **ADD** carbonated beverage and chill in dessert dishes until set, about 3 hours.

MAKES 4 servings.

SUGGESTED COMBINATIONS:

- Lime Gelatin Dessert with ginger ale.
- Orange Gelatin Dessert with root beer.
- Cherry Gelatin Dessert with cola.

***TIP:** Cool down the gelatin mixture until room temperature before adding the carbonated beverage if you wish to maintain the carbonation.*

CREATE-A-PUDDING SNACK

Prep time: 10 minutes   Chill time: 30 minutes

1 pkg	(4-serving size) JELL-O Instant Pudding & Pie Filling, any flavor	**1 pkg**
½ cup	mini or crumbled cookies, crushed fruit, mini-marshmallows	**125 mL**

▼ **PREPARE** pudding as directed on package.

▼ **STIR** in cookies, fruit or marshmallows.

▼ **SPOON** into individual dessert dishes. Chill 30 minutes.

MAKES 6 servings.

TIP: *A fun party idea. Let the kids make their own.*

Above: Create-A-Pudding Snack

Fun and Easy Pudsicles

Prep time: 5 minutes Freezing time: 4 hours or overnight

JELL-O Pudding or Gelatin Snacks, any flavor

- ▼ **INSERT** spoon or popsicle stick through foil cover of pudding or gelatin.
- ▼ **FREEZE** until firm, about 4 hours or overnight. Peel away foil top. Run warm water over popsicles for a few seconds to loosen plastic container.
- ▼ **DIP** in toppings of your choice, if desired or eat plain.

TIP: *Remove foil lid and stir in jam, chopped candy bars or chopped cookies. Place stick in cup and freeze. If desired, remove stick and container after freezing, and cover with thawed COOL WHIP Whipped Topping for a quick dessert.*

Above: Fun and Easy Pudsicles

FUN AND EASY SNACK CUPS

Prep time: 5 minutes

JELL-O Pudding Snacks, any flavor

- **STIR** chopped fruit, such as bananas or stawberries into your favorite snack cup flavor just before serving.
- **STIR** chocolate chips, chopped or mini cookies, chopped candy bars, mini marshmallows or sprinkles into your favorite snack cup flavor just before serving.

TIP: *Create your own pudding snack—use your imagination.*

Above: Fun and Easy Snack Cups

DESSERT EXPRESS

JELL-O Pudding Snacks, any flavor

- **EASY FONDUE:** Heat 1 pudding snack in microwave oven on medium power for 1 minute or until warm. Serve with a selection of fruit, marshmallows and cake.
- **EASY MOUSSE:** Fold ½ cup (125 mL) thawed COOL WHIP Whipped Topping into 1 chocolate pudding snack. Spoon into serving dish.

MAKES 1 serving.

- **ICY PUDDING TREAT:** Serve your favorite flavor of pudding with your favorite flavor of ice cream for a taste sensation.

TIP: *Give your kids a separate bag with pudding 'stir-ins' for their lunch.*

Above: Easy Fondue, Easy Mousse, Icy Pudding Treat

Peanut Butter and Grape Jell-O® Pie

Prep time: 50 minutes   Chill time: 3 hours or overnight

1 cup	milk	**250 mL**
½ cup	Smooth Peanut Butter	**125 mL**
1 pkg	(4-serving size) JELL-O Vanilla Instant Pudding & Pie Filling	**1 pkg**
2½ cups	thawed COOL WHIP Whipped Topping, divided	**625 mL**
1	prepared graham cracker crumb crust (6 ounces)	**1**
1 pkg	(4-serving size) JELL-O Grape Gelatin Dessert	**1 pkg**
¾ cup	boiling water	**175 mL**
2 cups	ice cubes	**500 mL**

▼ **STIR** milk gradually into peanut butter in medium bowl until smooth. Add pudding mix. Beat with wire whisk until smooth, about 2 minutes. Gently stir in 1 cup (250 mL) whipped topping.

▼ **SPOON** mixture into bottom of crumb crust. Refrigerate.

▼ **DISSOLVE** Gelatin Dessert in boiling water. Add ice cubes and stir until slightly thickened, about 3 to 5 minutes. Remove any unmelted ice. Whisk in remaining whipped topping. Chill until mixture is slightly thickened, about 30 minutes.

▼ **SPOON** mixture onto peanut butter mixture in crumb crust. Refrigerate 3 hours or overnight.

MAKES 8 servings.

TIP: *Freeze pie overnight, if desired. Let stand on counter 10 minutes before serving.*

DID YOU KNOW ABOUT PEANUT BUTTER:

From extra creamy to crunchy use the one of your choice. Did you know that 2 Tbsp (25 mL) of peanut butter contains 6.5 g of protein. It's also a good source of folacin plus niacin and thiamine.

Chocolate Candy Bar Dessert

Prep time: 20 minutes   Chill time: 2 hours

2 cups	chocolate wafer crumbs	**500 mL**
½ cup	butter, melted	**125 mL**
8 oz	PHILADELPHIA Cream Cheese, softened	**250 g**
¼ cup	granulated sugar	**50 mL**
4 cups	thawed COOL WHIP Whipped Topping	**1 L**
1 cup	chopped chocolate-covered crisp butter toffee bars (about 5 bars)	**250 mL**
3 cups	cold milk	**750 mL**
2 pkg	(4-serving size) JELL-O Chocolate Instant Pudding & Pie Filling	**2 pkg**

▼ **COMBINE** crumbs with butter. Press firmly onto bottom of 13 x 9 inch (33 x 23 cm) baking pan. Chill.

▼ **MIX** cream cheese and sugar in medium bowl with electric mixer until smooth. Gently stir in ½ of the whipped topping. Spread evenly over crust. Sprinkle chopped candy bars over cream cheese layer.

▼ **POUR** milk into a large bowl. Add pudding mixes. Beat with wire whisk on low speed of electric mixer for 2 minutes. Pour over chopped candy bar layer. Let stand 5 minutes or until thickened.

▼ **SPREAD** remaining whipped topping over pudding layer.

▼ **REFRIGERATE** 2 hours or until firm. Garnish with additional chopped candy bars, if desired. Cut into squares. Store leftover dessert in refrigerator.

MAKES 15 to 18 servings.

TIP: *For easy chopping of candy bars, leave in wrapper and break gently with the "handle" of a knife.*

Raspberry Smoothie

Prep time: 5 minutes   Chill time: 15 minutes

1 pkg	(4-serving size) JELL-O Raspberry Gelatin Dessert	**1 pkg**
1 cup	boiling water	**250 mL**
2 cups	vanilla ice cream	**500 mL**

▼ **DISSOLVE** Gelatin Dessert in boiling water.

▼ **ADD** ice cream by spoonfuls, whisking until smooth. Chill 15 minutes, or until mixture is slightly thickened.

▼ **SPOON** into dessert dishes.

▼ **CHILL** until set.

MAKES 4 servings.

TIP: *Serve with fresh raspberries, if desired.*

Opposite page: Peanut Butter and Grape JELL-O® Pie, Chocolate Candy Bar Dessert

AMBROSIA PARFAIT

Prep time: 20 minutes   Chill time: 30 minutes

1 pkg	(4-serving size) JELL-O Vanilla Instant Pudding & Pie Filling	**1 pkg**
1 cup	cold milk	**250 mL**
1 cup	crushed pineapple, undrained	**250 mL**
1	small banana, chopped	**1**
1 cup	miniature marshmallows	**250 mL**
1 can	(10 oz/284 mL) mandarin orange sections, drained	**1 can**
½ cup	sliced almonds, toasted	**125 mL**
½ cup	BAKER'S ANGEL FLAKE Coconut	**125 mL**

▼ **PREPARE** pudding as directed on package reducing milk to 1 cup (250 mL).

▼ **STIR IN** pineapple, banana and ½ cup (125 mL) of the marshmallows.

▼ **SPOON** one-third of the pudding mixture into 6 parfait glasses. Layer remaining ingredients, alternating with layers of pudding.

▼ **CHILL** until ready to serve, about 30 minutes.

MAKES 6 servings.

TIP: *Substitute 2 peeled and sectioned (membranes removed) fresh oranges for the mandarins, if desired.*

Above: Ambrosia Parfait, Raspberry Smoothie

Mocha Chocolate Delight Pie

Prep time: 15 minutes Cooking time: 10 minutes Chill time: 3 hours

1 pkg	(6-serving size) JELL-O Chocolate Pudding and Pie Filling	**1 pkg**
2 tsp	instant coffee granules	**10 mL**
1	prepared graham cracker crumb crust (6 ounces)	**1**
2 cups	thawed COOL WHIP Whipped Topping	**500 mL**

▼ **PREPARE** pudding mix as directed on package; stir in coffee. Cool 5 minutes, stirring twice.

▼ **MEASURE** 1 cup (250 mL) pudding; cover with waxed paper. Chill until cool, about ½ hour.

▼ **SPOON** remaining pudding into crumb crust. Cover with waxed paper. Chill.

▼ **BEAT** measured filling until smooth; fold into 1½ cups (375 mL) whipped topping. Spread over pudding in crumb crust. Chill 3 hours. Garnish with remaining whipped topping.

MAKES 8 servings.

TIP: *Eliminate coffee and substitute 1 Tbsp (15 mL) grated orange rind, if desired.*

Above from left to right: Rocky Road & Cookies'n Cream Ice Cream Shop Pies, Mocha Chocolate Delight Pie

COOKIES'N CREAM ICE CREAM SHOP PIE

Prep time: 15 minutes Freezing time: 6 hours or overnight

1½ cups	cold milk or half and half cream	**375 mL**
1 pkg	(4-serving size) JELL-O Vanilla Instant Pudding & Pie Filling	**1 pkg**
3½ cups	thawed COOL WHIP Whipped Topping	**875 mL**
1 cup	chopped chocolate sandwich cookies	**250 mL**
1	prepared graham cracker crumb crust (6 ounces)	**1**

- **POUR** milk into large bowl. Add pudding mix. Beat with wire whisk until well blended, 1 to 2 minutes. Let stand 5 minutes or until slightly thickened.
- **FOLD** whipped topping and chopped cookies into pudding mixture. Spoon into crumb crust.
- **FREEZE** pie until firm, about 6 hours or overnight. Remove from freezer. Let stand at room temperature about 10 minutes before serving to soften. Store any leftover pie in freezer.

MAKES 8 servings.

TIP: *For a lighter version, use JELL-O Sugar free Instant Pudding & Pie Filling and COOL WHIP LITE Whipped Topping. If desired, chill pie for 3 hours and serve.*

ROCKY ROAD ICE CREAM SHOP PIE

Prep time: 15 minutes Freezing time: 6 hours or overnight

1½ cups	cold milk or half and half cream	**375 mL**
1 pkg	(4-serving size) JELL-O Chocolate Instant Pudding & Pie Filling	**1 pkg**
3½ cups	thawed COOL WHIP Whipped Topping	**875 mL**
½ cup	**each** BAKER'S Semi-Sweet Chocolate Chips, miniature marshmallows and chopped nuts	**125 mL**
1	prepared graham cracker crumb crust (6 ounces)	**1**

- **POUR** milk into large bowl. Add pudding mix. Beat with wire whisk until well blended, 1 to 2 minutes. Let stand 5 minutes or until slightly thickened.
- **FOLD** whipped topping, chocolate chips, marshmallows and nuts into pudding mixture. Spoon into crumb crust.
- **FREEZE** pie until firm, about 6 hours or overnight. Remove from freezer. Let stand at room temperature about 10 minutes before serving to soften. Store leftover pie in freezer.

MAKES 8 servings.

TIP: *For best results when folding, use a rubber spatula. If desired, chill pie for 3 hours and serve.*

ORANGES TO GO

Prep time: 15 minutes   Chill time: 30 minutes

4	large oranges	**4**
1 pkg	(4-serving size) JELL-O Orange Gelatin Dessert	**1 pkg**
1 cup	boiling water	**250 mL**
2 cups	vanilla ice cream	**500 mL**

▼ **CUT** oranges in half. Remove fruit from each half. Scrape shells clean with a metal spoon. Finely chop fruit, removing membrane and set aside.

▼ **DISSOLVE** Gelatin Dessert in boiling water. Add ice cream by spoonfuls, stirring until smooth.

▼ **CHILL** until mixture is slightly thickened, about 15 minutes. Fold in chopped fruit.

▼ **SPOON** into orange shells. Chill until set, about 30 minutes.

MAKES 8 servings.

TIP: *Use fresh orange juice for the boiling liquid, if desired.*

Above: Oranges To Go

Above: Microwave Apple Bread Pudding, Dessert Nachos

MICROWAVE APPLE BREAD PUDDING

Prep time: 5 minutes Microwave cooking time: 13 minutes

6	slices raisin bread	**6**
2½ cups	milk	**625 mL**
1 pkg	(6-serving size) JELL-O Vanilla Pudding & Pie Filling	**1 pkg**
2	eggs, beaten	**2**
½ cup	raisins	**125 mL**
2	medium apples, peeled and chopped	**2**
¼ cup	packed brown sugar	**50 mL**
½ tsp	ground cinnamon	**2 mL**

- **CUT** bread into ½ inch (1 cm) cubes and set aside.
- **GRADUALLY WHISK** milk into pudding mix in a large microwavable bowl.
- **COOK** on HIGH power for 5 minutes, stirring twice. Add eggs, stirring well and continue to cook on HIGH power another 3 minutes, stirring once.
- **STIR** in raisins and apples. Cook 4 minutes more stirring once. Gently stir in bread cubes and cook another minute.
- **BLEND** sugar and cinnamon. Sprinkle over pudding. Serve warm.

MAKES 6 to 8 servings.

***TIP:** Use white bread, if desired.*

DESSERT NACHOS

Prep time: 20 minutes

20	graham crackers	**20**
1 pkg	(4-serving size) JELL-O Vanilla Instant Pudding & Pie Filling	**1 pkg**
2 cups	strawberries, sliced	**500 mL**
3	kiwi, chopped	**3**
1	large banana, sliced	**1**
	Chocolate sauce	

- **SCORE** each graham cracker diagonally with knife; break apart to form 2 triangles.
- **PREPARE** pudding as directed on package.
- **DIVIDE** graham cracker triangles evenly among 8 dessert plates. Spoon pudding over the triangles. Top with fruit.
- **DRIZZLE** with chocolate sauce. Serve immediately.

MAKES 8 servings.

***TIP:** Create your own flavor combination of pudding and fruit as desired. A fun party idea. Have all components made and let people create their own "nachos".*

STRIPE IT RICH

Prep time: 30 minutes ***Baking time: 20 minutes*** ***Chill time: 2 to 3 hours***

1¼ cups	all-purpose flour	**300 mL**
¾ cup	finely chopped pecans	**175 mL**
½ cup	granulated sugar, divided	**125 mL**
½ cup	butter, melted	**125 mL**
8 oz	PHILADELPHIA Cream Cheese, softened	**250 g**
3 cups	cold milk, divided	**750 mL**
4 cups	thawed COOL WHIP Whipped Topping	**1 L**
2 pkg	(4-serving size) JELL-O Chocolate Instant Pudding & Pie Filling	**2 pkg**
	Chocolate curls (optional)	

- **COMBINE** flour, pecans, ¼ cup (50 mL) of the sugar and butter until moist. Press mixture evenly into bottom of 13 x 9 inch (33 x 23 cm) pan. Bake at 350°F (180°C) for 20 minutes or until lightly golden. Cool on rack.
- **BEAT** cream cheese with remaining ¼ cup (50 mL) sugar and 2 Tbsp (25 mL) of the milk until smooth. Fold in half of the topping. Spread over cooled crust.
- **POUR** the remaining milk into a large bowl. Add pudding mixes. Beat with wire whisk until well blended, about 2 to 3 minutes scraping bowl occasionally. Pour over cream cheese layer. Chill 2 to 3 hours.
- **CUT** into servings and garnish each with the remaining topping. Add chocolate curls, if desired.

MAKES 16 servings.

TIP: *Dessert may be frozen for up to 1 week. Thaw in refrigerator.*

DID YOU KNOW ABOUT* COOL WHIP *WHIPPED TOPPING:

COOL WHIP comes in Regular or Lite (low in fat). Both products may be interchanged in these recipes, if desired. Remember, COOL WHIP Whipped Topping may be re-frozen if your recipe doesn't use the entire container or use it to top your favorite dessert.

CHOCOLATE WAFER-ORANGE DESSERT

Prep time: 15 minutes   Chill time: 3 hours or overnight

18	chocolate wafers	**18**
1 pkg	(4-serving size) JELL-O Vanilla Instant Pudding & Pie Filling	**1 pkg**
1 cup	milk	**250 mL**
1 cup	thawed COOL WHIP Whipped Topping	**250 mL**
2	medium oranges, peeled and thinly sliced	**2**
3 Tbsp	orange marmalade	**45 mL**
1 tsp	water	**5 mL**

▼ **ARRANGE** half the cookies in bottom of 8 inch (20 cm) square pan.

▼ **PREPARE** pudding mix with 1 cup (250 mL) milk as directed on package. Fold in whipped topping.

▼ **POUR** half the pudding mixture over cookies in pan. Layer remaining cookies and remaining pudding mixture. Top with orange slices.

▼ **THIN** marmalade with water; spoon over oranges. Chill about 3 hours. Cut into squares.

MAKES 9 servings.

TIP: *Use JELL-O Chocolate Instant Pudding & Pie Filling instead of Vanilla, if desired.*

Above: Stipe It Rich, Chocolate Wafer-Orange Dessert

Quick Parfait

Prep time: 20 minutes   Chill time: 1 hour

¾ cup	boiling water	**175 mL**
1 pkg	(4-serving size) JELL-O Raspberry Sugar Free Gelatin Dessert or your favorite flavor	**1 pkg**
½ cup	cold water	**125 mL**
	Ice cubes	
½ cup	thawed COOL WHIP or COOL WHIP LITE Whipped Topping	**125 mL**

- **POUR** boiling water into blender container. Add Gelatin Dessert and blend at low speed until dissolved, about 30 seconds.
- **COMBINE** cold water and ice cubes to make 1¼ cups (300 mL). Add to gelatin and stir until ice is partially melted, then blend at high speed for 10 seconds. Add whipped topping and blend 15 seconds.
- **POUR** mixture into straight-sided parfait glasses. Chill until set, about 1 hour.

MAKES about 3 cups (750 mL) or 6 servings.

TIP: *Scrape down sides of blender to ensure all gelatin is dissolved, using a rubber spatula.*

PER SERVING:
Calories 26, Protein 1 g, Fat 1.6 g, Carbohydrate 1.5 g

Applestick Snack

Prep time: 5 minutes   Chill time: 1 hour

1 pkg	(4-serving size) JELL-O Strawberry Sugar Free Gelatin Dessert	**1 pkg**
1 cup	boiling water	**250 mL**
½ cup	apple juice	**125 mL**
1 cup	ice cubes	**250 mL**
1	medium unpeeled red, yellow or green apple, cut in sticks	**1**

- **DISSOLVE** Gelatin Dessert in boiling water. Add apple juice and ice cubes stirring until gelatin is slightly thickened. Remove any unmelted ice. Add apple.
- **SPOON** into serving dishes. Chill until set, about 1 hour.

MAKES 4 servings.

TIP: *Substitute Bosc or Bartlett pear "sticks" for the apple, if desired.*

PER SERVING:
Calories 43, Protein 1.5 g, Fat 0.2 g, Carbohydrate 9.1 g, Dietary Fiber 0.7 g

Opposite page: Applestick Snack, Quick Parfait, JELL-O® Sparkle

LAYERED FRUIT DESSERT

Prep time: 20 minutes

2 cups	strawberry halves	**500 mL**
2	peaches, peeled, cubed	**2**
1 cup	fresh blueberries	**250 mL**
2 cups	seedless green grapes, halved	**500 mL**
1 pkg	(4-serving size)JELL-O Vanilla Instant Sugar Free Pudding & Pie Filling	**1 pkg**
2 cups	milk (2 %)	**500 mL**
½ cup	yogurt, plain or fruit flavored	**125 mL**

▼ **LAYER** fruits in medium glass serving bowl or individual parfait dishes.

▼ **PREPARE** pudding as directed on package. Fold in yogurt. Spoon over fruit.

▼ **SERVE** immediately.

MAKES 4 servings, ½ cup (125 mL) each.

TIP: *Substitute 6 cups (1.5 L) unsweetened drained canned fruit for the fresh.*

PER SERVING:
Calories 225, Protein 7.2 g, Fat 4.1 g, Carbohydrate 43.2 g, Dietary Fiber 4.4 g

DID YOU KNOW ABOUT YOGURT:

Yogurt is a cultured milk, much like buttermilk, sour cream, and crème fraîche. It develops from the action of bacteria. Calories and nutrients differ from brand to brand, use low fat yogurt for less fat.

CHOCOLATE ANGEL DESSERT

Prep time: 15 minutes   Chill time: 15 minutes

1½ cups	small angel food cake cubes	**375 mL**
1 cup	raspberries, sliced strawberries or sliced bananas	**250 mL**
1½ cups	cold milk (2 %)	**375 mL**
1 pkg	(4-serving size) JELL-O Chocolate Instant Sugar Free Pudding & Pie Filling	**1 pkg**
1 cup	thawed COOL WHIP LITE Whipped Topping	**250 mL**

▼ **DIVIDE** cake cubes and fruit evenly among 6 dessert dishes; set aside.

▼ **POUR** milk into medium bowl; add pudding mix. Beat with wire whisk 1 to 2 minutes or until well blended. Let stand 5 minutes.

▼ **GENTLY** fold in whipped topping. Spoon into dessert dishes. Chill 15 minutes.

MAKES 6 servings.

Quick and Easy Light Jell-O Mousse *- Ready in 5 minutes! Prepare Instant Pudding & Pie Filling according to package directions. Stir in 1½ cups (375 mL) thawed COOL WHIP LITE Whipped Topping. Spoon into dessert dishes.*

PER SERVING:
Calories 109, Protein 3.3 g, Fat 3.1 g, Carbohydrate 18 g, Dietary Fiber 1.0 g

Above from left to right: Layered Fruit Dessert, Chocolate Angel Dessert

Above: Fruit Terrine Supreme

FRUIT TERRINE SUPREME

Prep time: 20 minutes   Chill time: 4 hours

Fruit Terrine

2 pkg	(4-serving size) JELL-O Lemon Sugar Free Gelatin Dessert	**2 pkg**
1½ cups	boiling water	**375 mL**
¾ cup	orange juice	**175 mL**
	Ice cubes	
2 tsp	grated orange rind	**10 mL**
4 cups	thawed COOL WHIP LITE Whipped Topping	**1 L**

Blueberry Sauce

10 oz	frozen unsweetened blueberries, thawed	**300 g**
2 Tbsp	lemon juice	**25 mL**
⅓ cup	sugar or equivalent artificial sweetener	**75 mL**
2 Tbsp	water	**25 mL**

FRUIT TERRINE:

- ▼ **DISSOLVE** Gelatin Dessert in boiling water. Combine orange juice and ice cubes to make 1¾ cups (425 mL). Add to gelatin, stirring until ice is melted. Stir in orange rind. Chill until slightly thickened.
- ▼ **FOLD** topping into gelatin mixture. Spoon into 9 x 5 inch (23 x 13cm) loaf pan. Chill 4 hours or overnight. To unmold dip in warm water for 15 seconds and invert onto cutting board or serving platter. Slice and serve with Blueberry Sauce.

MAKES 10 servings.

BLUEBERRY SAUCE:

- ▼ **COMBINE** blueberries, lemon juice, sugar and water in medium saucepan. (If using artificial sweetener add last.) Bring to a boil.
- ▼ **COOK** and stir over medium heat for 2 to 3 minutes. Process in food processor or blender for 1 minute until smooth. (Add sweetener to taste.) Chill. Stir well before serving. Makes about 1 cup (250 mL).

TIP: *Substitute unsweetened frozen or fresh strawberries or raspberries for the blueberries, if desired.*

PER SERVING:
Calories 157, Protein 1.7 g, Fat 8.3 g, Carbohydrate 19.9 g, Dietary Fiber 1.0 g

DID YOU KNOW HOW TO PROTECT YOUR BAKING PANS:

For metal baking pans, wash in hot soapy water, rinse well. Place in a warm (200° F/95° C) oven. Turn off oven and leave ½ hour to dry. This will prevent rusting and will also prevent color from 'leaching' into food. If your pans are already 'old', line with plastic wrap for non-baked desserts.

LIGHT'N FRUITY STRAWBERRY PIE

Prep time: 20 minutes Chill time: 3 hours

1 pkg	(4-serving size) JELL-O Strawberry Sugar Free Gelatin Dessert	**1 pkg**
2/3 cup	boiling water	**150 mL**
2 cups	ice cubes	**500 mL**
4 cups	thawed COOL WHIP LITE Whipped Topping	**1 L**
1 cup	crushed fresh strawberries	**250 mL**
1	prepared graham cracker crumb crust (6 ounces)	**1**

▼ **DISSOLVE** Gelatin Dessert in boiling water. Add ice cubes and stir constantly until gelatin starts to thicken, 3 to 5 minutes. Remove any unmelted ice.

▼ **WHISK** in whipped topping gently until smooth. Fold in fruit. Chill until thick, about 15 minutes.

▼ **SPOON** into crust. Chill 3 hours.

MAKES 8 servings.

TIP: *For Raspberry Pie, substitute with JELL-O Raspberry Sugar Free Gelatin Dessert and raspberries for the strawberries.*

PER SERVING:
Calories 198, Protein 2.2 g, Fat 10.1 g, Carbohydrate 26 g, Dietary Fiber 0.9 g

Above: Light'n Fruity Strawberry Pie

Light Lemon Cheesecake

Prep time: 15 minutes   Chill time: 4 hours

3 Tbsp	graham cracker crumbs	**45 mL**
1 pkg	(4-serving size) JELL-O Lemon Sugar Free Gelatin Dessert	**1 pkg**
2/3 cup	boiling water	**150 mL**
16 oz	Light PHILADELPHIA Cream Cheese	**500 g**
	Grated rind of 2 lemons	
	Juice of 1 lemon	
2 cups	thawed COOL WHIP LITE Whipped Topping	**500 mL**

- **SPRINKLE** crumbs onto sides of 8 inch (20 cm) springform pan which has been sprayed with nonstick cooking spray.
- **PLACE** Gelatin Dessert in blender container. Add water; blend on low speed until dissolved. Add cream cheese; blend at medium speed until smooth, scraping sides of blender. Pour into large bowl.
- **FOLD** in lemon rind, juice and topping. Pour into prepared pan; smooth top. Chill 4 hours. Serve with fresh fruit.

MAKES 12 servings.

TIP: *For easier squeezing of lemons, have at room temperature and roll lemon on counter lightly before squeezing.*

PER SERVING:
Calories 154, Protein 4.1 g, Fat 12.8 g, Carbohydrate 6 g, Dietary Fiber 0.1 g

Above: Light Lemon Cheesecake

Above: Cherry Waldorf Salad, Fiesta Carrot Pineapple Salad

CHERRY WALDORF SALAD

Prep time: 10 minutes   Chill time: 30 minutes

1 pkg	(4-serving size) JELL-O Cherry Sugar Free Gelatin Dessert	**1 pkg**
¾ cup	boiling water	**175 mL**
½ cup	cold water	**125 mL**
	Ice cubes	
½ cup	unpeeled diced apple	**125 mL**
1	small banana, sliced	**1**
¼ cup	sliced celery	**50 mL**

▼ **DISSOLVE** Gelatin Dessert in boiling water. Combine cold water and ice cubes to make 1¼ cups (300 mL). Add to gelatin and stir until slightly thickened; remove any unmelted ice.

▼ **FOLD** in fruits and celery. Chill in individual dishes until set, about 30 minutes. Makes about 2½ cups (625 mL) or 5 servings.

TIPS: *Substitute 1 orange, peeled and sectioned, for the banana, if desired.*
Pour into a 4 cup (1 L) mold and chill 3 hours, if desired. Unmold and serve.

PER SERVING:
Calories 32, Protein 1.5 g, Fat 0.1 g, Carbohydrate 6.4 g, Dietary Fiber 0.6 g

FIESTA CARROT PINEAPPLE SALAD

Prep time: 2 hours   Chill time: 2 hours or overnight

1 pkg	(4-serving size) JELL-O Lemon Sugar Free Gelatin Dessert	**1 pkg**
1 cup	boiling water	**250 mL**
1 can	(14 oz/398 mL) pineapple tidbits in own juice	**1 can**
½ cup	shredded carrot	**125 mL**

▼ **DISSOLVE** Gelatin Dessert in boiling water. Drain pineapple tidbits reserving liquid; add cold water to measure 1 cup (250 mL); stir into gelatin.

▼ **CHILL** gelatin until slightly thickened, about 1¼ hours.

▼ **STIR** in pineapple tidbits and shredded carrots. Pour into 4 cup (1 L) bowl. Chill until set.

MAKES 6 servings.

TIP: *Pour gelatin mixture into lightly greased muffin cups, chill and unmold for individual servings.*

PER SERVING:
Calories 51, Protein 1.3 g, Fat 0.1 g, Carbohydrate 12 g, Dietary Fiber 0.8 g

Above: Very Berry, Sunshine Squeeze

VERY BERRY

Prep time: 15 minutes Chill time: 30 minutes

1 pkg	(4-serving size) JELL-O Strawberry Sugar Free Gelatin Dessert	**1 pkg**
1 cup	thawed COOL WHIP LITE Whipped Topping	**250 mL**
1 cup	fresh sliced strawberries	**250 mL**

- **PREPARE** Gelatin Dessert according to 30 Minute Set Method on package. Measure ½ cup (125 mL) of gelatin. Whisk into topping. Spoon into dessert dishes. Chill 20 minutes.
- **MEANWHILE,** fold strawberries into remaining gelatin. Spoon over bottom layer. Chill until set, about 30 minutes.

MAKES 4 servings.

TIP: *To prepare slanted dessert, lean empty parfait glasses against the rim of a square pan. Secure with tape and support underneath with folded paper towel. Prepare creamy layer as above and spoon into glasses. Chill as above. Stand upright and spoon fruited gelatin over bottom layer. Chill until set.*

PER SERVING:
Calories 79, Protein 1.8 g, Fat 4.9 g, Carbohydrate 7.1 g, Dietary Fiber 0.8 g

SUNSHINE SQUEEZE

Prep time: 15 minutes Chill time: 30 minutes

1 pkg	(4-serving size) JELL-O Orange Sugar Free Gelatin Dessert	**1 pkg**
1 cup	orange sections	**250 mL**

- **PREPARE** Gelatin Dessert according to 30 Minute Set Method on package.
- **SET ASIDE** ½ cup (125 mL). Chill until slightly thickened.
- **FOLD** orange sections into remaining gelatin. Spoon into 6 dessert dishes.
- **BEAT** reserved gelatin with mixer until double in volume. Spoon over fruited layer. Chill until set, about 30 minutes.

MAKES 4 servings.

TIP: *For best volume when beating gelatin, place in a small bowl and beat at high speed with an electric mixer.*

PER SERVING:
Calories 29, Protein 1.8 g, Fat 0.1 g, Carbohydrate 5.4 g, Dietary Fiber 0.8 g

DID YOU KNOW ABOUT ORANGES:

Low in calories and sodium and high in vitamin C. Oranges come in many varieties from Blood oranges to Temple oranges. They should be firm and heavy for their size when purchased, smooth and unblemished. Store at room temperature for 3 to 4 days or in plastic bags in the refridgerator.

Above: Amazing Melon Wedge, Light Fruit Treasure Cup

AMAZING MELON WEDGE

Prep time: 10 minutes Chill time: 3 hours

1	medium melon	**1**
1 pkg	(4-serving size) JELL-O Lime Sugar Free Gelatin Dessert	**1 pkg**

- **CUT** melon in half lengthwise; scoop out seeds; drain well. Dry inside with paper towel.
- **PREPARE** Gelatin Dessert according to 30 Minute Set Method on package.
- **PLACE** melon halves in small bowls and spoon gelatin into centers. Chill until firm, about 3 hours. To serve, cut in wedges or slices.

MAKES 6 servings.

TIP: *Use any flavor of JELL-O. Use cantaloupe or honeydew, if desired.*

PER SERVING:
Calories 81, Protein 1.9 g, Fat 0.2 g, Carbohydrate 19.7 g, Dietary Fiber 1.7 g

LIGHT FRUIT TREASURE CUP

Prep time: 5 minutes Chill time: 30 minutes

1 pkg	(4-serving size) JELL-O Strawberry Sugar Free Gelatin Dessert	**1 pkg**
1 can	(14 oz/398 mL) fruit cocktail, drained	**1 can**
1 cup	low fat cottage cheese	**250 mL**

- **PREPARE** Gelatin Dessert according to 30 Minute Set Method on package.
- **STIR** fruit cocktail into slightly thickened gelatin.
- **DIVIDE** cottage cheese among 4 dessert dishes. Top with fruit gelatin mixture. Chill until set, about 30 minutes.

MAKES 4 servings.

TIP: *Substitute plain yogurt for the cottage cheese, if desired.*

PER SERVING:
Calories 87, Protein 9.5 g, Fat 0.6 g, Carbohydrate 10.3 g, Dietary Fiber 0.8 g

DID YOU KNOW ABOUT PREVENTING FRUIT FROM BROWNING:

Fruits such as sliced apples, pears, peaches, and bananas will brown when exposed to the air. Sprinkle with orange, lemon or lime juice to prevent browning.

Above: Fruited Squares, Foamy Peach Snack

FRUITED SQUARES

Prep time: 10 minutes   Chill time: 3 hours

2 pkg	(4-serving size) JELL-O Strawberry Sugar Free Gelatin Dessert or your favorite flavor	**2 pkg**
1½ cups	boiling water	**375 mL**
1 cup	cold water	**250 mL**
2 cups	thawed COOL WHIP or COOL WHIP LITE Whipped Topping	**500 mL**
1 can	(14 oz/398 mL) fruit cocktail in fruit juice or light syrup, drained*	**1 can**

* or use 1 cup (250 mL) sliced fresh fruit.

▼ **DISSOLVE** Gelatin Dessert in boiling water. Combine cold water and ice cubes to make 2 cups (500 mL). Add to gelatin and stir until slightly thickened; remove any unmelted ice. Measure 1 cup (250 mL) and fold into whipped topping; pour into 8 inch (20 cm) square pan.

▼ **ARRANGE** fruit on creamy layer, then spoon remaining gelatin over fruit. Chill until firm, about 3 hours. Cut into 9 squares.

MAKES 9, ½ cup (125 mL) servings.

TIP: *Variations - Raspberry or strawberry Gelatin Dessert with sliced pineapple or peaches.*
- Cherry or lime Gelatin Dessert with sliced banana or pears.
- Orange Gelatin Dessert with apricot halves.

PER SERVING (1 square):
Calories 75, Protein 1.6 g, Fat 4.2 g, Carbohydrate 7.7 g, Dietary Fiber 0.3 g

FOAMY PEACH SNACK

Prep time: 10 minutes   Chill time: 1 hour

1 can	(14 oz/398 mL) sliced peaches, in fruit juice	**1 can**
1 pkg	(4-serving size) JELL-O Raspberry Sugar Free Gelatin Dessert	**1 pkg**
½ cup	ice cubes	**125 mL**

▼ **DRAIN** peaches, reserving juice. Add water to juice to make ¾ cup (175 mL); bring measured liquid to a boil.

▼ **POUR** boiling liquid into blender container. Add Gelatin Dessert and blend at low speed until dissolved, about 1 minute.

▼ **ADD** ice cubes and blend at low speed until ice is partially melted. Add peaches and blend at high speed until ice is melted, about 30 seconds.

▼ **POUR** into 6 dessert dishes. Chill until set, about 1 hour.

MAKES 6 servings.

TIP: *Substitute 1 cup (250 mL) fresh raspberries for the peaches, if desired.*

PER SERVING:
Calories 36, Protein 1.4 g, Fat 0 g, Carbohydrate 8.1 g, Dietary Fiber 0.7 g

STRAWBERRY YOGURT FLUFF

Prep time: 5 minutes   Chill time: 1 hour

¾ cup	boiling water	**175 mL**
1 pkg	(4-serving size) JELL-O Strawberry Sugar Free Gelatin Dessert	**1 pkg**
½ cup	cold water	**125 mL**
	Ice cubes	
1 cup	plain, low fat yogurt	**250 mL**
	Fresh strawberries for garnish (optional)	

▼ **POUR** boiling water into blender container. Add Gelatin Dessert and blend at low speed until dissolved, about 1 minute.

▼ **COMBINE** cold water and ice cubes to make 1 cup (250 mL). Add to gelatin and stir until ice is almost melted. Remove unmelted ice. Blend in yogurt.

▼ **CHILL** in dessert dishes until set, about 1 hour. If desired, garnish with fresh strawberries.

MAKES 4 servings.

TIP: *For best results when dissolving gelatin powder in blender, scrape sides with rubber spatula after 1 minute.*

PER SERVING:
Calories 39, Protein 3.5 g, Fat 1.2 g, Carbohydrate 3 g

Above: Strawberry Yogurt Fluff

TRADITIONAL FRUIT TRIFLE

Prep time: 30 minutes   Chill time: 2 hours or overnight

Gelatin layer

4 cups	pound cake cubes	**1 L**
2 Tbsp	sweet sherry	**25 mL**
1 can	(14 oz/398 mL) fruit cocktail, drained	**1 can**
1 pkg	(4-serving size) JELL-O Strawberry Gelatin Dessert	**1 pkg**

Custard layer

1 pkg	(4-serving size) JELL-O Vanilla Pudding & Pie Filling	**1 pkg**
2 Tbsp	sweet sherry	**25 mL**
2 cups	thawed COOL WHIP Whipped Topping	**500 mL**

GELATIN LAYER:

▼ **PLACE** cake cubes in large 10 cup (2.5 L) serving bowl; sprinkle with sherry. Add fruit cocktail.

▼ **PREPARE** Gelatin Dessert according to 30 Minute Set Method on package. Spoon slightly thickened gelatin over fruit cocktail; chill until set.

CUSTARD LAYER:

▼ **PREPARE** pudding and pie filling mix as directed on package increasing milk to 2½ cups (625 mL). Add sherry. Cover with plastic wrap; chill. Measure ⅔ cup (150 mL) whipped topping; set aside.

▼ **FOLD** pudding into remaining whipped topping. Spoon over gelatin in bowl. Chill at least 2 hours.

▼ **GARNISH** with reserved whipped topping. If desired, garnish with nuts and candied cherries.

MAKES 8 to 10 servings.

***TIP**: Trifle may be made up to 2 days ahead. If desired, substitute 2 cups (500 mL) chopped fresh fruit for the fruit cocktail.*

DID YOU KNOW ABOUT MAKING* BAKER'S *CHOCOLATE CURLS:

Warm the chocolate slightly until the texture is pliable enough to curl. Chocolate can be warmed by holding the wrapped square in the palm of your hand until chocolate softens slightly, or microwave on DEFROST for approximately 1 minute per square. When the chocolate is slightly softened and pliable, carefully draw a vegatable peeler over the smooth surface of the square. Use a toothpick to gently lift the curls without breaking them.

Cherry Topped Eggnog Ring

Prep time: 1 hour   Chill time: 4 hours or overnight

1 can	(284 mL) mandarin orange segments	**1 can**
1 pkg	(4-serving size) JELL-O Cherry or Cranberry Gelatin Dessert	**1 pkg**
1 cup	boiling water	**250 mL**
1 cup	chopped apple	**250 mL**
1 pkg	(4-serving size) JELL-O Lemon Gelatin Dessert	**1 pkg**
1 cup	boiling water	**250 mL**
¾ cup	canned or dairy eggnog	**175 mL**
¼ cup	cold water	**50 mL**
1 tsp	dark rum (optional)	**5 mL**
2 cups	thawed COOL WHIP Whipped Topping	**500 mL**

▼ **DRAIN** mandarin oranges, measuring syrup. Add water to syrup to make 1 cup (250 mL).

▼ **DISSOLVE** cherry Gelatin Dessert in 1 cup (250 mL) boiling water. Add measured liquid. Chill until slightly thickened, about 1¼ hours. Add mandarin oranges and apples.

▼ **SPOON** into a large 6 cup (1.5 L) gelatin mold. Chill.

▼ **MEANWHILE,** dissolve lemon Gelatin Dessert in 1 cup (250 mL) boiling water. Cool to room temperature Add eggnog, cold water and rum. Chill until slightly thickened, about 1¼ hours.

▼ **FOLD** eggnog mixture into 1 cup (250 mL) whipped topping. Spoon over fruit gelatin layer in mold.

▼ **CHILL** until set, about 4 hours or overnight. Unmold onto chilled serving plate. Garnish with remaining topping.

MAKES 10 servings.

TIP: *Garnish with sugar coated cherries, if desired. To sugar coat, beat 1 egg white until frothy. Dip cherries in the egg white and then in granulated sugar.*

Opposite page: Traditional Fruit Trifle

Above: Cherry Topped Eggnog Ring

Above: Gingerbread People, Microwave Popcorn Balls

Gingerbread People

Prep time: 20 minutes   Baking time: 10 to 12 minutes

1 pkg	(6-serving size) JELL-O Butterscotch Pudding & Pie Filling	**1 pkg**
¾ cup	butter	**175 mL**
¾ cup	firmly packed brown sugar	**175 mL**
1	egg	**1**
2¼ cups	all-purpose flour	**550 mL**
1 tsp	baking soda	**5 mL**
1 Tbsp	ground ginger	**15 mL**
1½ tsp	ground cinnamon	**7 mL**

▼ **CREAM** pudding and pie filling mix with butter and sugar. Add egg and blend well.

▼ **COMBINE** flour, baking soda, ginger and cinnamon; blend into pudding mixture. Chill dough until firm, about 1 hour.

▼ **ROLL** on a floured board to about ¼ inch (0.5 cm) thickness and cut with cookie cutter.

▼ **PLACE** on greased baking sheets; use a straw to make a hole in the top of the cookie for hanging on the tree.

▼ **BAKE** at 350°F (180°C) for 10 to 12 minutes. Remove from oven and cool on wire rack. Decorate as desired.

MAKES 16 to 18 gingerbread cookies.

TIP: *Small icing tubes are ideal for decorating cookies.*

Microwave Popcorn Balls

Prep time:10 minutes

¼ cup	butter	**50 mL**
6 cups	miniature marshmallows	**1500 mL**
1 pkg	(4-serving size) JELL-O Gelatin Dessert, any flavor	**1 pkg**
12 cups	popped popcorn	**3 L**
1 cup	peanuts (optional)	**250 mL**

▼ **PLACE** butter and marshmallows in large microwavable bowl. Cook in microwave on HIGH power for 1½ to 2 minutes or until marshmallows are puffed.

▼ **ADD** dry Gelatin Dessert; stir until well blended.

▼ **POUR** marshmallow mixture over combined popcorn and peanuts. Stir quickly to coat well.

▼ **SHAPE** into balls, teddy bears or other shapes with greased hands. Decorate as desired.

MAKES about 36 popcorn balls.

TIP: *Substitute raisins for the peanuts, if desired. Work quickly when combining marshmallow mixture and popcorn as mixture will thicken.*

Above: Family Favorite Nanaimo Bars, Cappuccino Cups

Family Favorite Nanaimo Bars

Prep time: 30 minutes   Chill time: 3 hours

3 squares	BAKER'S Unsweetened Chocolate	**3 sq**
½ cup	butter	**125 mL**
1½ cups	graham cracker crumbs	**375 mL**
½ cup	finely chopped toasted pecans	**125 mL**
1 pkg	(4-serving size) JELL-O Vanilla Instant Pudding & Pie Filling	**1 pkg**
⅓ cup	**each:** butter and boiling water	**75 mL**
2 cups	powdered sugar	**500 mL**
3 squares	BAKER'S Semi-Sweet Chocolate	**3 sq**
½ cup	whipping cream	**125 mL**

▼ **MELT** unsweetened chocolate and ½ cup (125 mL) butter over low heat; remove. Add crumbs and pecans; mix well.

▼ **PRESS** into 9 inch (23 cm) square pan. Chill.

▼ **COMBINE** pudding mix, ⅓ cup (75 mL) butter and water; blend in powdered sugar until smooth. Spread over crust; chill until set, about 1 hour.

▼ **MELT** semi-sweet chocolate and cream over low heat; stir until smooth. Spread over pudding layer. Chill.

▼ **STORE** in refrigerator; let stand at room temperature 30 minutes before slicing. Sprinkle with powdered sugar, if desired.

MAKES 24 bars.

TIP: *Use any flavor of pudding, as desired. Store in an airtight container in refrigerator up to 1 week.*

Cappuccino Cups

Prep time: 15 minutes   Freeze time: 6 hours

12	chocolate wafers	**12**
2 Tbsp	instant coffee granules	**25 mL**
¼ cup	hot water	**50 mL**
1½ cups	half and half cream or milk	**375 mL**
1 pkg	(4-serving size) JELL-O Vanilla Instant Pudding & Pie Filling	**1 pkg**
¼ tsp	ground cinnamon	**1 mL**
3½ cups	thawed COOL WHIP Whipped Topping	**875 mL**
2 squares	BAKER'S Semi-Sweet Chocolate, melted	**2 sq**

▼ **PLACE** 1 cookie in bottom of 12 paper-lined muffin cups.

▼ **DISSOLVE** instant coffee in hot water in medium bowl. Add cream, pudding mix and cinnamon. Beat with whisk about 2 minutes. Let stand 5 minutes or until slightly thickened.

▼ **FOLD** in whipped topping. Spoon into muffin cups. Freeze until firm, about 6 hours.

▼ **REMOVE** dessert from paper cup. Place on individual dessert plate. Drizzle melted chocolate over each dessert cup.

MAKES 12 individual cups.

TIP: *Garnish with chocolate covered coffee beans, if desired.*

Above: Easy Grasshopper Pie, Cherry Revel

Easy Grasshopper Pie

Prep time: 20 minutes   Chill time: 3 hours or overnight

1 pkg	(4-serving size) JELL-O Lime Gelatin Dessert	**1 pkg**
2/3 cup	boiling water	**150 mL**
2 cups	ice cubes	**500 mL**
1 cup	thawed COOL WHIP Whipped Topping	**250 mL**
2 Tbsp	Creme de Menthe liqueur	**25 mL**
1	prepared graham cracker crumb crust (6 ounces)	**1**

▼ **DISSOLVE** Gelatin Dessert in boiling water. Add ice cubes and stir constantly until gelatin starts to thicken, about 3 to 5 minutes. Remove any unmelted ice.

▼ **ADD** whipped topping and liqueur to gelatin and whisk until well blended.

▼ **SPOON** into crumb crust. Chill 3 hours. Garnish with lime slices or mint leaves, if desired.

MAKES 8 servings.

TIP: *If you don't have Creme de Menthe, substitute 1 tsp (5 mL) mint extract and several drops green food coloring.*

Cherry Revel

Prep time: 30 minutes   Chill time: 4 hours or overnight

3 squares	BAKER'S Semi-Sweet Chocolate, chopped	**3 sq**
2 pkg	(4-serving size) JELL-O Cherry Gelatin Dessert	**2 pkg**
2 cups	boiling water	**500 mL**
4 cups	ice cubes	**1 L**
4 cups	thawed COOL WHIP Whipped Topping	**1 L**
1 cup	cherry pie filling	**250 mL**
3 squares	BAKER'S Semi-Sweet Chocolate (for garnish)	**3 sq**
	Maraschino cherries with stems	

▼ **MELT** chocolate in microwavable bowl on MEDIUM power about 2 minutes. Stir until smooth. Drizzle chocolate on inside of 8 to 10 cup (2 to 2.5 L) glass bowl using a spoon. Refrigerate bowl.

▼ **DISSOLVE** Gelatin Dessert in boiling water. Add ice and stir until gelatin begins to thicken. Remove any unmelted ice. Whisk in 3 cups (750 mL) whipped topping and chill until mixture is slightly thickened, about 20 minutes. Fold in cherry pie filling and spoon into glass bowl. Chill 4 hours or overnight.

▼ **JUST** before serving, garnish top with remaining topping, chocolate curls and cherries.

MAKES 10 to 12 servings.

TIP: *Cool chocolate slightly to prevent running down sides of bowl.*

TRUFFLE TREATS

Prep time: 15 minutes   Freeze time: 4 hours or overnight

6 squares	BAKER'S Semi-Sweet Chocolate	**6 sq**
¼ cup	butter	**50 mL**
7 oz	BAKER'S ANGEL FLAKE Coconut	**200 g**
8 oz	PHILADELPHIA Cream Cheese, softened	**250 g**
2½ cups	milk or half and half cream	**625 mL**
1 pkg	(4-serving size) JELL-O Instant Chocolate Pudding & Pie Filling	**1 pkg**
1 cup	thawed COOL WHIP Whipped Topping	**250 mL**
2 squares	BAKER'S Semi-Sweet Chocolate, grated	**2 sq**

▼ **LINE** a 13 x 9 inch (33 x 23 cm) baking pan with waxed paper to extend over the sides of the pan.

▼ **HEAT** chocolate and butter over low heat or in microwave on MEDIUM power for 2 minutes, until butter is melted. Stir until completely smooth; reserve 2 Tbsp (25 mL).

▼ **STIR** chocolate into coconut; toss to coat evenly. Press mixture into baking pan.

▼ **BEAT** cream cheese at medium speed of electric mixer until smooth; beat in reserved chocolate. Gradually beat in milk.

▼ **ADD** pudding mix. Beat at low speed until well blended, about 2 minutes. Gently fold in whipped topping. Pour over crust. Sprinkle with grated chocolate, pressing lightly. Freeze until firm, about 4 hours or overnight.

▼ **REMOVE** from freezer. Run knife around outside. Lift from pan onto cutting board. Removed waxed paper. Cut into diamonds, squares or triangles. Store leftover treats in the refrigerator or freezer.

MAKES about 20 treats.

***TIP:** Sprinkle squares with powdered sugar, if desired.*

***DID YOU KNOW ABOUT* PHILADELPHIA CREAM CHEESE:**

Cream cheese originated in Chester, New York in 1872 and is made from a combination of milk and cream which gives it a special smooth richness. Cream cheese is a fresh cheese which is moist, unripened, and unfermented. Philadelphia Cream Cheese produced by Kraft is one of the best known of all cream cheeses. Cream cheese can be plain or spiced or seasoned. It is best used as spreads, dips, sauces or in desserts such as cheesecakes.

Opposite page: Easy Tiramisu, Truffle Treats

EASY TIRAMISU

Prep time: 30 minutes ***Cook time: 10 minutes*** ***Chill time: 4 hours***

1 pkg	(6-serving size) JELL-O Vanilla Pudding & Pie Filling	**1 pkg**
8 oz	PHILADELPHIA Cream Cheese, softened	**250 g**
¼ cup	coffee liqueur	**50 mL**
1 Tbsp	instant coffee granules	**15 mL**
½ cup	hot water	**125 mL**
1 Tbsp	granulated sugar	**15 mL**
1 pkg	(7 oz/200 g) lady fingers	**1 pkg**
1½ cups	thawed COOL WHIP Whipped Topping	**375 mL**
4 squares	BAKER'S Semi-Sweet Chocolate, coarsely grated	**4 sq**

▼ **PREPARE** pudding mix according to package directions. Beat cream cheese and coffee liqueur into hot filling. Cover with plastic wrap and chill 1 hour.

▼ **COMBINE** coffee granules, hot water and sugar; brush over lady fingers.

▼ **FOLD** whipped topping into pudding mixture.

▼ **LINE** bottom of 8 cup (2 L) trifle bowl with ½ of the lady fingers. Spread ½ of pudding mixture over lady fingers; sprinkle with ½ of the grated chocolate. Repeat layers. Cover tightly; chill 4 hours or overnight to blend flavors.

MAKES 10 to 12 servings.

DID YOU KNOW ABOUT GRATING* BAKER'S *CHOCOLATE:

Use a fine or coarse grater. For larger pieces, use a coarse grater and warm the chocolate as you would for chocolate curls. Grate chocolate onto a piece of waxed paper. A food processer with a grating disc works well too.

LEMON CHEESE PIE

Prep time: 25 minutes Chill time: 3 hours

1	baked 9 inch (23 cm) pastry crust	**1**
1 pkg	(4-serving size) JELL-O Lemon Pudding & Pie Filling	**1 pkg**
½ cup	granulated sugar	**125 mL**
1¼ cups	water	**300 mL**
2	egg yolks	**2**
1 cup	milk	**250 mL**
4 oz	PHILADELPHIA Cream Cheese, softened	**125 g**
1 Tbsp	butter	**15 mL**
2	egg whites	**2**
¼ cup	granulated sugar	**50 mL**

- **CHILL** baked crust.
- **COMBINE** pudding and pie filling mix, ½ cup (125 mL) sugar and ¼ cup (50 mL) of the water in saucepan. Blend in egg yolks, remaining 1 cup (250 mL) water and milk.
- **COOK,** stirring constantly, over medium heat until mixture comes to a full bubbling boil.
- **BEAT** cream cheese in a small bowl until smooth. Beat ½ of pie filling into cheese. Stir butter into remaining ½ of pie filling.
- **BEAT** egg whites until foamy throughout. Gradually beat in ¼ cup (50 mL) sugar and continue beating until mixture forms stiff shiny peaks.
- **FOLD** egg whites into lemon-cheese mixture. Spread evenly in baked pie crust. Chill 5 minutes.
- **SPOON** remaining pie filling evenly over filling in pie crust. Chill 3 hours before serving.

MAKES about 8 servings.

TIP: *For extra lemon flavor, substitute 2 Tbsp (25 mL) lemon juice for 2 Tbsp (25) water and add 1 tsp (5 mL) grated lemon rind to pudding.*

LEMON COCONUT BARS

Prep time: 20 minutes   Baking time: 50 to 60 minutes

½ cup	butter	**125 mL**
¼ cup	powdered sugar	**50 mL**
1¼ cups	all-purpose flour	**300 mL**
2	eggs	**2**
½ cup	granulated sugar	**125 mL**
1 pkg	(4-serving size) JELL-O Lemon Pudding & Pie Filling	**1 pkg**
½ tsp	baking powder	**2 mL**
1 cup	chopped dates	**250 mL**
1½ cups	BAKER'S ANGEL FLAKE Coconut	**375 mL**
	powdered sugar	

▼ **CREAM** butter and powdered sugar. Add flour and mix well.

▼ **PRESS** evenly into bottom of 8 inch (20 cm) square pan.

▼ **BAKE** at 350°F (180°C) for 20 to 25 minutes, until lightly browned.

▼ **MEANWHILE,** beat eggs until thick and light in color. Gradually beat in granulated sugar.

▼ **BLEND** in pudding and pie filling mix and baking powder. Fold in dates and coconut.

▼ **SPREAD** over hot baked crust. Return to oven and bake 30 to 35 minutes longer, until golden brown. Cool.

▼ **SPRINKLE** with powdered sugar if desired; cut into bars. Store in tightly covered container.

MAKES 1 to 1½ dozen bars.

__TIP:__ Substitute dried apricots for the dates, if desired.

DID YOU KNOW ABOUT DATES:

To cut dates easily, dip the knife or kitchen scissors in hot water occasionally to prevent sticking. Store in an airtight container in the refrigerator for freshness.

Opposite page: Lemon Coconut Bars, Lemon Cheese Pie

Above: Sparkling Fruits in Strawberry-Kiwi JELL-O®, shown with vanilla pudding

Sparkling Fruits In Strawberry-Kiwi Jell-O®

Prep time: 40 minutes   Chill time: 3 hours or overnight

Crust

1½ cups	graham cracker crumbs	**375 mL**
⅓ cup	butter, melted	**75 mL**
¼ cup	granulated sugar	**50 mL**

Bottom Layer

2 pkg	(4-serving size) JELL-O Strawberry-Kiwi or Lemon Gelatin Dessert	**2 pkg**
2 cups	boiling water	**500 mL**
3 cups	vanilla ice cream	**750 mL**

Top Layer

	Sliced strawberries and lime rind slices for stems	
2 pkg	(4-serving size) JELL-O Strawberry-Kiwi or Lemon Gelatin Dessert	**2 pkg**
1 cup	boiling water	**250 mL**
1 cup	cold water	**250 mL**

CRUST:

▼ **COMBINE** crumbs, butter and sugar; press onto base of a 9 inch (23 cm) springform pan. Chill.

BOTTOM LAYER:

▼ **DISSOLVE** Gelatin Desserts in boiling water. Whisk spoonfuls of ice cream into gelatin until smooth. Chill 15 minutes. Whisk again until smooth. Pour into prepared pan. Chill 45 minutes.

TOP LAYER:

▼ **DECORATIVELY** arrange fruit on bottom layer which should be set but still sticky. Chill while preparing clear layer.

▼ **DISSOLVE** Gelatin Desserts in boiling water. Stir in cold water. Chill 15 minutes. Gently spoon a thin layer of gelatin over fruit. Chill pan 10 minutes. Spoon on remainder of gelatin. Chill 3 hours.

MAKES 10 to 12 servings.

__TIP:__ Substitute 30 Minute-Set Method for __TOP LAYER__, if desired. Dissolve Gelatin Desserts in 1⅓ cups (300 mL) boiling water. Add 2 cups (500 mL) ice cubes and stir until gelatin is slightly thickened. Remove unmelted ice. Stir in 1 cup (250 mL) sliced strawberries. Spoon over ice cream layer. Chill 3 hours or overnight.

Front cover photo

Above: Fluffy Cranberry Orange Pie,
Creamy Lemon Cups

Creamy Lemon Cups

Prep time: 15 minutes   Chill time: 4 hours or overnight

2 pkg	(4-serving size) JELL-O Lemon Gelatin Dessert	**2 pkg**
2 cups	boiling water	**500 mL**
½ cup	cold water	**125 mL**
1½ cups	cold milk	**375 mL**
1 pkg	(4-serving size) JELL-O Vanilla Instant Pudding & Pie Filling	**1 pkg**
½ tsp	ground nutmeg	**2 mL**
2 cups	thawed COOL WHIP Whipped Topping	**500 mL**

▼ **DISSOLVE** Gelatin Dessert in boiling water. Stir in cold water. Cool to room temperature.

▼ **POUR** milk into another bowl. Add pudding mix. Beat with wire whisk 30 seconds. Immediately stir into cooled gelatin until smooth. Stir in nutmeg. Refrigerate about 1½ hours or until slightly thickened.

▼ **STIR** in whipped topping with wire whisk until smooth and creamy. Pour into 10 individual dessert dishes or drinking mugs.

▼ **REFRIGERATE** 4 hours or until firm. Garnish with additional whipped topping and sprinkle with additional ground nutmeg just before serving.

MAKES 10 servings.

TIP: *Cut top from lemons. Remove fruit from each. Scrape shells clean with a metal spoon. Fill with lemon mixture. Chill.*

Fluffy Cranberry Orange Pie

Prep time: 30 minutes   Chill time: 3 hours or overnight

1 pkg	(4-serving size) JELL-O Cranberry Gelatin Dessert	**1 pkg**
1 cup	boiling water	**250 mL**
2 cups	ice cubes	**500 mL**
3 cups	thawed COOL WHIP Whipped Topping	**750 mL**
¾ cup	whole cranberry sauce	**175 mL**
1 tsp	grated orange rind	**5 mL**
1	prepared graham cracker crumb crust (6 ounces)	**1**
	Sugared cranberries - optional	
	Orange slices, cut into small wedges	

▼ **DISSOLVE** Gelatin Dessert in boiling water, stirring until completely dissolved, about 2 minutes. Add ice cubes. Stir until gelatin thickens about 3 to 5 minutes. Remove any unmelted ice.

▼ **FOLD** gelatin into 2½ cups (625 mL) whipped topping; blend until smooth. Fold in cranberry sauce and orange rind.

▼ **REFRIGERATE** 20 minutes or until mixture is thick.

▼ **SPOON** into crumb crust. Refrigerate 3 hours.

▼ **GARNISH** with remaining whipped topping, sugared cranberries and orange slices.

MAKES 8 servings.

TIP: *Dip fresh cranberries into lightly beaten egg white; roll in sugar in flat plate to coat well. Place on tray covered with waxed paper.*

Triple Chocolate Almond Pudding Cake

Prep time: 20 minutes   Baking time: 55 to 60 minutes

Cake

1 pkg	(2-layer size) Devil's Food or chocolate cake mix	**1 pkg**
1 pkg	(4-serving size) JELL-O Chocolate Instant Pudding & Pie Filling	**1 pkg**
1 cup	sour cream or plain yogurt	**250 mL**
½ cup	vegetable oil	**125 mL**
½ cup	water	**125 mL**
½ cup	toasted chopped almonds	**125 mL**
4	eggs	**4**
3 Tbsp	almond liqueur or 1 tsp (5 mL) almond extract	**45 mL**
1 cup	BAKER'S Semi-Sweet Chocolate Chips	**250 mL**

Glaze

4 squares	BAKER'S Semi-Sweet Chocolate	**4 sq**
2 Tbsp	butter	**25 mL**
2 Tbsp	almond liqueur	**25 mL**
½ tsp	vegetable oil	**2 mL**

CAKE:

▼ **PLACE** all ingredients, except chocolate chips in large mixer bowl and beat for 4 minutes at medium speed. Stir in chocolate chips. Pour into 10 inch (25 cm) greased and floured tube or fluted tube pan.

▼ **BAKE** at 350°F (180°C) for 55 to 60 minutes or until cake springs back when lightly pressed. Let cool in pan for 15 minutes. Remove from pan and leave on rack until completely cooled.

GLAZE:

▼ **MELT** chocolate with butter over hot water. Stir in liqueur and oil. Spoon over cake. Garnish with toasted slivered almonds and chocolate curls, if desired.

MAKES 10 to 12 servings.

***TIP**: Instead of flour, use cocoa powder to dust pan for a darker color to cake. Substitute a 13 x 9 inch (33 x 23 cm) cake pan, if desired. Adjust baking time.*

Opposite page: Triple Chocolate Almond Pudding Cake

Above: Merry-Go-Round Cake

Merry-Go-Round Cake

Prep time: 30 minutes   Baking time: 50 minutes

1 pkg	(6-serving size) JELL-O Vanilla Instant Pudding & Pie Filling	**1 pkg**
1 pkg	(2-layer size) yellow cake mix	**1 pkg**
4	eggs	**4**
1 cup	water	**250 mL**
¼ cup	vegetable oil	**50 mL**
⅔ cup	cold milk	**150 mL**
	Sprinkles (optional)	
	Colored paper and plastic straws	
	Animal crackers	

- **RESERVE** ⅓ cup (75 mL) pudding mix.
- **COMBINE** cake mix, remaining pudding mix, eggs, water and oil in large bowl. Beat at low speed of electric mixer just to moisten, scraping sides of bowl often. Beat at medium speed 4 minutes.
- **POUR** batter into greased and floured 10 inch (25 cm) fluted tube pan.
- **BAKE** at 350°F (180°C) for 50 minutes or until cake tester inserted in center comes out clean. Cool in pan 15 minutes. Remove from pan; finish cooling on rack.
- **BEAT** reserved pudding mix and milk in a small bowl until smooth. Spoon over top of cake to glaze. Garnish with sprinkles, if desired.
- **CUT** 10 to 12 inch (25 to 30 cm) circle from colored paper; scallop edges, if desired. Make 1 slit to center. Overlap cut edges together to form carousel roof; secure with tape. Cut straws in half; insert around top of cake. Arrange animal crackers at base of straws. Top with roof.

MAKES 12 servings.

TIP: *Use JELL-O Chocolate Instant Pudding & Pie Filling and a chocolate cake mix, if desired.*

Melon Angel Mousse

Prep time: 20 minutes   Chill time: 4 hours or overnight

2 pkg	(4-serving size) JELL-O Strawberry-Kiwi or Watermelon Gelatin Dessert	**2 pkg**
2 cups	**each** boiling water and ice cubes	**500 mL**
4 cups	thawed COOL WHIP Whipped Topping	**1 L**
1	(200 g) Angel Food cake, cut in small cubes	**1**
1 cup	**each** cubed canteloupe and honeydew melon	**250 mL**

- **DISSOLVE** Gelatin Dessert in boiling water. Add ice cubes, stirring until gelatin thickens, about 3 to 5 minutes.
- **FOLD** in half of topping; add cake and melon.
- **POUR** into 6 cup (1.5 L) bowl lined with plastic wrap.
- **CHILL** 4 hours or overnight.
- **UNMOLD** onto serving plate; remove plastic. Frost with remaining whipped topping; garnish with additional melon, if desired.

MAKES 10 to 12 servings.

TIP: *Dessert can be made 2 days in advance of serving.*

Above: Melon Angel Mousse

Celebration Squares

Prep time: 30 minutes ***Chill time: 30 minutes***

1 cup	graham cracker crumbs	**250 mL**
¼ cup	melted butter	**50 mL**
8 oz	PHILADELPHIA Cream Cheese, softened	**250 g**
¼ cup	granulated sugar	**50 mL**
4 cups	thawed COOL WHIP Whipped Topping	**1 L**
2 pkg	(4-serving size) JELL-O Cherry or Strawberry Gelatin Dessert	**2 pkg**
1 can	(14 oz/398 mL) crushed pineapple, drained	**1 can**
1 square	BAKER'S Semi-Sweet Chocolate, melted	**1 sq**

- **MIX** together crumbs and butter. Press firmly in bottom of 13 x 9 inch (33 x 23 cm) baking pan. Refrigerate.
- **BEAT** cream cheese and sugar until smooth. Gently fold in half of the topping. Spread over crust.
- **PREPARE** Gelatin Dessert according to 30 Minute Set Method on package.
- **IMMEDIATELY** stir drained fruit into gelatin. Spoon over cream cheese layer.
- **REFRIGERATE** 30 minutes. Spread remaining topping over gelatin.
- **DECORATE** with "maple leaf" jigglers, if desired - see Jiggler recipe, page 23.

MAKES 20 pieces.

TIP: *Soften cream cheese on DEFROST setting in the microwave for 2 minutes.*

DID YOU KNOW ABOUT STAR FRUIT:

Also called carambola, this is a bright yellow to green, deeply grooved, oval fruit the size of an orange. Sliced horizontally, the fruit looks like a five sided 'star'. They should be juicy and crisp in texture with a refreshing taste somewhat similar to a plum.

SANGRIA SPLASH RING

Prep time: 30 minutes   Chill time: 4 hours or overnight

2 pkg	(4-serving size) JELL-O Lemon Gelatin Dessert	**2 pkg**
1½ cups	boiling dry white wine	**375 mL**
2 cups	chilled club soda	**500 mL**
1 Tbsp	orange liqueur (optional)	**15 mL**
3 cups	fruit: sliced strawberries, sliced star fruit, green and red grapes	**750 mL**
	Additional fruit for garnish	

▼ **DISSOLVE** Gelatin Desserts in boiling wine in medium bowl. Let cool to room temperature.

▼ **STIR** in club soda and liqueur. Chill until gelatin is slightly thickened.

▼ **FOLD** in 3 cups (750 mL) fruit. Pour into 6 cup (1.5 L) mold or loaf pan. Chill 4 hours or overnight.

▼ **TO UNMOLD,** dip mold in warm water for about 10 seconds. Gently pull gelatin from around edges with moist fingers. Place moistened serving plate on top of mold. Invert mold and plate; holding mold and plate together, shake slightly to loosen. Gently remove mold and center gelatin on plate. Garnish with additional fruit.

MAKES 12 servings.

TIP: *Grease mold slightly with vegetable oil for easier removal.*

Opposite page: Celebration Squares

Above: Sangria Splash Ring

BUMBLEBERRY PIE

Prep time: 30 minutes   Chill time: 3 hours

1 pkg	(4-serving size) JELL-O Strawberry Gelatin Dessert	**1 pkg**
2/3 cup	boiling water	**150 mL**
2 cups	ice cubes	**500 mL**
4 cups	thawed COOL WHIP Whipped Topping	**1 L**
1/3 cup	**each** mashed strawberries, whole raspberries and blueberries	**75 mL**
1	prepared graham cracker crumb crust (6 ounces)	**1**
	Aditional fruit for garnish, if desired	

▼ **DISSOLVE** Gelatin Dessert in boiling water.

▼ **ADD** ice cubes and stir until gelatin starts to thicken about 3 to 5 minutes. Remove any unmelted ice.

▼ **BLEND** topping into gelatin. Fold in fruit.

▼ **CHILL** until mixture is slightly thickened, about 15 minutes. Spoon into crumb crust. Chill for 3 to 4 hours.

▼ **JUST** before serving, garnish with additional fruit, if desired.

MAKES 8 servings.

TIP: *Pie may be frozen 1 week. Thaw in refrigerator.*

Above: Bumbleberry Pie

Raspberry Glazed Lemon Mousse Cake

Prep time: 30 minutes   Chill time: 4 hours

27	ice wafers	**27**
8 oz	PHILADELPHIA Cream Cheese, softened	**250 g**
	Juice and rind of 1 lemon	
2 pkg	(4-serving size) JELL-O Lemon Gelatin Dessert	**2 pkg**
1¼ cups	boiling water	**300 mL**
2 cups	ice cubes	**500 mL**
4 cups	thawed COOL WHIP Whipped Topping	**1 L**
½ cup	fresh raspberries	**125 mL**
1 pkg	(4-serving size) JELL-O Raspberry Gelatin Dessert	**1 pkg**
1 cup	**each** boiling water and ice cubes	**250 mL**

- **GREASE** a 9 inch (23 cm) springform pan. Place wafers around inside rim. Set aside.
- **BEAT** cream cheese in large bowl of electric mixer. Add lemon juice and rind, beating on low speed until blended.
- **DISSOLVE** lemon Gelatin Dessert in boiling water. Add ice cubes; stirring until slightly thickened, about 3 to 5 minutes. Remove unmelted ice.
- **ADD** gelatin slowly to cream cheese mixture while beating on low speed. Increase speed and beat just until well blended.
- **FOLD** in whipped topping. Pour into prepared pan. Arrange raspberries on top and chill.
- **DISSOLVE** raspberry Gelatin Dessert in boiling water; add ice cubes and stir until slightly thickened. Immediately spoon over cake. Chill 4 hours.

MAKES 10 to 12 servings.

TIP: *For a lighter dessert substitute light cream cheese, COOL WHIP LITE Whipped Topping and JELL-O Sugar Free Gelatin Dessert for regular products.*

DID YOU KNOW ABOUT ICE CUBES:

Ice cubes come in many shapes and sizes. This will effect your gelatin set when using the 30 Minute Set Method. All sizes will work but your gelatin may be slightly softer or firmer depending upon the shape you use.

Pear Terrine

Prep time: 15 minutes   Chill time: 4 hours or overnight

2 pkg	(4-serving size) JELL-O Lemon Gelatin Dessert	**2 pkg**
2 cups	boiling water	**500 mL**
1½ cups	cold water	**375 mL**
1 Tbsp	lemon juice	**15 mL**
1 can	(14 oz/398 mL) pear halves, drained	**1 can**
8 oz	PHILADELPHIA Cream Cheese, softened	**250 g**
¼ tsp	ground ginger	**1 mL**

- **DISSOLVE** Gelatin Desserts in boiling water. Add cold water and lemon juice. Measure 2 cups (500 mL) into 9 x 5 inch (23 x 13 cm) loaf pan. Chill until set, but not firm (gelatin should be sticky to the touch), about 2 hours. Leave remaining gelatin at room temperature.
- **MEANWHILE** finely chop pears and set aside.
- **BEAT** cheese until creamy. Very slowly whisk in remaining gelatin, whisking until smooth. Blend in ginger.
- **CHILL** until slightly thickened. Stir in pears. Spoon over gelatin in pan. Chill until firm 4 hours or overnight.
- **UNMOLD** on crisp lettuce and slice.

MAKES 10 servings.

TIP: *If remaining gelatin sets too firm, heat to soften.*

Sunset Salad

Prep time: 10 minutes   Chill time: 4 hours or overnight

2 pkg	(4-serving size) JELL-O Orange or Lemon Gelatin Dessert	**2 pkg**
½ tsp	salt	**2 mL**
1½ cups	boiling water	**375 mL**
1 can	(14 oz/398 mL) crushed pineapple with juice, undrained	**1 can**
1 Tbsp	lemon juice	**15 mL**
1 cup	grated carrots	**250 mL**

- **DISSOLVE** Gelatin Dessert and salt in boiling water. Add pineapple with juice and lemon juice. Chill until slightly thickened about 45 minutes.
- **FOLD** in carrots. Pour into an 8 inch (20 cm) square pan. Chill until firm about 4 hours.
- **TO SERVE,** cut in squares and place on salad greens.

MAKES 8 to 10 servings.

TIP: *Can also be poured into individual gelatin mold or greased muffin pan.*

Opposite page: Raspberry Glazed Lemon Mousse Cake

Above:Pear Terrine, Sunset Salad

FROZEN BANANA BOMBE

Prep time: 15 minutes   Freezing time: 4 hours or overnight

1 square	BAKER'S Semi-Sweet Chocolate, melted	**1 sq**
2	ripe bananas, mashed	**2**
1¼ cups	cold milk	**300 mL**
¼ cup	rum	**50 mL**
1 pkg	(4-serving size) JELL-O Vanilla Instant Pudding & Pie Filling	**1 pkg**
8 oz	PHILADELPHIA Cream Cheese, softened	**250 g**
2 cups	thawed COOL WHIP Whipped Topping	**500 mL**

- **LINE** a large glass bowl with plastic wrap. Drizzle inside with melted chocolate; freeze to set.
- **MASH** bananas; set aside.
- **PLACE** milk, rum, pudding mix and cream-cheese in large bowl. Beat with electric mixer on medium speed until smooth. Stir in bananas.
- **FOLD** in whipped topping; spoon into prepared bowl. Freeze until firm.
- **REMOVE** from freezer, unmold and remove plastic wrap. Let stand at room temperature 5 minutes before slicing to serve.

MAKES 8 servings.

TIP: *Substitute orange juice for the rum, if desired. Leftover COOL WHIP Whipped Topping may be refrozen.*

CHERRY ALMOND CHEESE SQUARES

Prep time: 20 minutes   Freezing time: 2 hours

40	graham crackers	**40**
16 oz	PHILADELPHIA Cream Cheese, softened	**500 g**
3 cups	cold milk, divided	**750 mL**
2 pkg	(4-serving size **each**) JELL-O Vanilla Instant Pudding & Pie Filling	**2 pkg**
1 tsp	almond extract	**5 mL**
2 cups	thawed COOL WHIP Whipped Topping	**500 mL**
1 can	(19 oz/540 mL) cherry pie filling	**1 can**

- **ARRANGE** half of the crackers on bottom of 13 x 9 inch (33 x 23 cm) pan, cutting to fit if necessary.
- **BEAT** cream cheese at low speed of electric mixer until smooth. Gradually beat in 1 cup (250 mL) of the milk. In another bowl, combine pudding mix, remaining 2 cups (500 mL) of the milk and almond extract; whisk until blended. Add to cream cheese mixture and blend well. Fold in whipped topping.
- **SPREAD** half of the pudding mixture over crackers. Arrange second layer of cookies on top. Top with remaining pudding mixture.
- **FREEZE** 2 hours. Let stand at room temperature 20 minutes before cutting into squares.
- **SPOON** cherry pie filling over each square.

MAKES 16 servings.

TIP: *Use chocolate pudding, if desired.*

Above: Cherry Almond Cheese Squares, Frozen Banana Bombe

JIGG-O-LANTERN

Prep time: 15 minutes   Chill time: 30 minutes

1 pkg	(4-serving size) JELL-O Orange Gelatin Dessert	**1 pkg**
1 cup	boiling water	**250 mL**
2 cups	vanilla ice cream, softened	**500 mL**
	assorted candies	

▼ **DISSOLVE** Gelatin Dessert in boiling water. Cool to room temperature.

▼ **ADD** ice cream by spoonfuls, whisking until smooth.

▼ **POUR** into dessert dishes. Chill until set, about 30 minutes.

▼ **MAKE** "pumpkin" faces on gelatin with candies.

Makes 4 servings.

***TIP:** Decorate with candies no more than 1 hour before serving or candies may "weep".*

WORM CAKES

Prep time: 30 minutes   Chill time: 3 hours

24	white cupcakes	**24**
1 pkg	(4-serving size) JELL-O Grape Gelatin Dessert	**1 pkg**
1 cup	boiling water	**250 mL**
2 cups	thawed COOL WHIP Whipped Topping	**500 mL**
	Gummy worms, chocolate wafer crumbs	

▼ **PLACE** cupcakes in muffin tins. Pierce cupcakes with a large fork at ¼ inch (.5 cm) intervals; about 3 to 5 times.

▼ **DISSOLVE** Gelatin Dessert in boiling water. Using a teaspoon carefully pour the gelatin over each cupcake.

▼ **REFRIGERATE** 3 hours. Dip muffin pan in warm water 10 seconds; unmold onto serving plate. Frost with whipped topping.

▼ **GARNISH** with gummy worms and wafer crumbs to resemble 'dirt'. Store frosted cupcakes in refrigerator.

MAKES 24 servings.

***TIP**: These can be made in advance and frozen for 1 week.*

Next page: Jigg-O-Lantern

Swamp Water

Prep time: 5 minutes

2 cups	cold milk	**500 mL**
1 pkg	(4-serving size) JELL-O Grape Gelatin Dessert	**1 pkg**
2½ cups	vanilla ice cream or frozen yogurt	**625 mL**

▼ **POUR** milk in blender. Add Gelatin Dessert and ice cream; cover.

▼ **BLEND** at high speed 30 seconds or until smooth.

▼ **POUR** into glasses. Serve immediately.

Makes about 4 cups (1 L).

TIP: *Freeze glasses for ½ hour before filling for "frosty" look.*

Above: Worm Cakes, Swamp Water

Above: Tombstone Squares

Tombstone Squares

Prep time: 30 minutes   Chill time: 2 hours or overnight

2½ cups	chocolate wafer crumbs, divided	**625 mL**
⅓ cup	melted butter	**75 mL**
2 pkg	(4-serving size) JELL-O Orange Gelatin Dessert	**2 pkg**
1½ cups	boiling water	**375 mL**
¾ cup	orange juice	**175 mL**
	Ice cubes	
4 cups	thawed COOL WHIP Whipped Topping	**1 L**
	Decorations: Assorted rectangular-shaped cookies, writing gels, colored coconut and candy	

- **MIX** 2 cups (500 mL) of the wafer crumbs and melted butter; press firmly into bottom of a 13 x 9 inch (33 x 23 cm) pan.
- **DISSOLVE** Gelatin Dessert in boiling water. Combine orange juice and ice cubes to make 1¾ cups (425 mL). Add to gelatin, stirring until ice is almost melted. Remove unmelted ice. Pour over crust. Chill until slightly thickened, about 1¼ hours.
- **TOP** with whipped topping.
- **SPRINKLE** remaining ½ cup (125 mL) wafer crumbs over whipped topping. Decorate cookies with icings to make "tombstones" and stand on top of dessert with coconut and candies to resemble a graveyard. Cut into squares.

MAKES 15 to 18 servings.

***TIP:** Small tubes of colored writing gels work well for writing on cookies and are available at most grocery stores.*

Dixie Spiders

Prep time: 15 minutes   Chill time: 2 hours

2 pkg	(4-serving size) JELL-O Grape Gelatin Dessert	**2 pkg**
1¼ cups	boiling water	**300 mL**
6	(3 oz /85 mL) paper cups	**6**
	Licorice allsorts or other decorating candies String licorice cut into 3 inch (7.5 cm) pieces	

- **DISSOLVE** Gelatin Dessert in boiling water, stirring until completely dissolved, about 2 minutes. Pour into paper cups.
- **REFRIGERATE** until firm, at least 2 hours.
- **CAREFULLY** peel away paper cups from gelatin. Slice a thin layer from long side to help 'spider' sit flat. Insert 3 licorice pieces on each side of spider for legs; place licorice allsorts on top for eyes.

MAKES 6 spiders.

***TIP:** For a fun kids party, let the children help in decorating their own 'spider'.*

Above: Dixie Spiders

WITCHES BREW

Prep time: 15 minutes Chill time: 2 hours

Hand

2 pkg	(4-serving size) JELL-O Grape Gelatin Dessert	**2 pkg**
1½ cups	boiling water	**375 mL**

Eye Balls

1 pkg	(4-serving size) JELL-O Orange Gelatin Dessert	**1 pkg**
¾ cup	boiling water	**175 mL**
¼ cup	whole blueberries	**50 mL**
	Prepared Orange KOOL-AID	

HAND

▼ **DISSOLVE** Gelatin Dessert in boiling water, stirring until completely dissolved, about 2 minutes.

▼ **POUR** into a greased 8 inch (20 cm) baking pan.

▼ **REFRIGERATE** until firm, about 2 hours.

▼ **TRACE** outline of a small hand on a piece of paper. Cut out the pattern and place on top of set gelatin. Using a knife, cut around the pattern. Carefully pull the 'hand' away from the baking pan.

▼ **PLACE** 'hand' in punch bowl; allowing 'fingers' to hang over sides of bowl.

EYE BALLS

▼ **DISSOLVE** Gelatin Dessert in boiling water, stirring until completely dissolved, about 2 minutes.

▼ **POUR** into round or square ice cube trays. Refrigerate until partially set. Poke a blueberry into the center of each gelatin eye ball; place in refrigerator until completely set.

▼ **PLACE** 'eye balls' around inside of punch bowl.

▼ **POUR** in prepared orange drink mix.

MAKES 10 to 12 servings.

TIP: *Use left over grape gelatin to make individual 'fingers' or cut into pieces and serve with fresh fruit.*

Above: Witches Brew

Crown Jewel Dessert

Prep time: 40 minutes   Chill time: 4 hours or overnight

1 pkg	(4-serving size) JELL-O Strawberry and Lime Gelatin Desserts	**1 pkg**
1 pkg	(4-serving size) JELL-O Strawberry-Kiwi Gelatin Dessert	**1 pkg**
3 cups	boiling water	**750 mL**
1½ cups	cold water	**375 mL**
1 pkg	(4.4 oz/125 g) 'bakery style' lady fingers	**1 pkg**
2 cups	thawed COOL WHIP Whipped Topping	**500 mL**

▼ **PREPARE** strawberry and lime Gelatin Desserts separately, as directed on package, reducing **cold** water to ½ cup (125 mL) for **each**. Pour **each** into an 8 inch (20 cm) square pan. Chill until set, about 1 hour.

▼ **PREPARE** strawberry-kiwi Gelatin Dessert as directed on package reducing **cold** water to ½ cup (125 mL). Chill until slightly thickened.

▼ **TRIM** length of one end of each lady finger to fit pan. Line the sides of 9 inch (23 cm) springform pan with cut lady fingers. (See tip below).

▼ **FOLD** whipped topping into slightly thickened strawberry-kiwi gelatin; gently fold in red and green gelatin cut into ½ inch (1 cm) cubes.

▼ **CAREFULLY** spoon into pan. Chill until firm, about 4 hours or overnight.

MAKES 12 servings.

TIPS: *DO NOT add fresh kiwi to gelatin as it will not set. Use your favorite flavors of JELL-O to create your own flavor combination, if desired.*

DID YOU KNOW ABOUT LADY FINGERS:

Lady fingers come in many different types. Types may be interchanged in recipes.

1. Giant Lady Fingers

A soft cookie type found in the cookie section of the grocery store. They come in 150 g (5.3 oz) packages.

2. Bakery Style Lady Fingers

They are found mostly in the bakery section of the grocery store. They are soft in texture. Packages usually contain 24 fingers.

3. Sugar Coated Biscuits (Champagne biscuits)

They are found in the baking or cookie section of the grocery store. These are crisp in texture. They come in packages of 24, about 400 g.

3. Ice Wafers

They are found in the cookie section of the grocery store and come in vanilla, chocolate or strawberry. Packages are 200 g and contain 21 wafers.

Opposite page: Crown Jewel Dessert

Above: Celebration Rainbow Cake

Celebration Rainbow Cake

Prep time: 10 minutes   Baking time: 30 minutes   Chill time: 4 hours

1 pkg	(2-layer size) white cake mix	**1 pkg**
2 pkg	(4-serving size) JELL-O Gelatin Dessert, any flavors	**2 pkg**
2 cups	boiling water	**500 mL**
4 cups	thawed COOL WHIP Whipped Topping	**1 L**
	Toasted flaked coconut (optional)	
	Gumdrops (optional)	

- **LINE** bottoms and grease sides of two 9 inch (23 cm) cake pans.
- **PREPARE** and bake cake mix as directed on package.
- **COOL** in pans 15 minutes; do not remove from pans.
- **DISSOLVE** each package of Gelatin Dessert separately in 1 cup (250 mL) boiling water.
- **POKE** cakes with fork at ½ inch (1 cm) intervals.
- **DRIZZLE** one flavor gelatin over one cake. Repeat with second cake layer and gelatin flavor. Chill 4 hours.
- **UNMOLD** one cake onto serving plate, cover with some of the whipped topping. Unmold second cake onto first. Frost top and sides with remaining whipped topping. Sprinkle with coconut and garnish with flattened gumdrops, if desired. Chill.

MAKES 10 servings.

TIP: *Flatten gumdrops with a rolling pin. Cut into flower petal shape. Roll one to make a tight "bud". Add 2 or more "petals" around center to make flower. Cut a green gum drop for "stem" and "leaves".*

Rainbow Ribbon

Prep time: 3 hours   Chill time: 4 hours or overnight

5 pkg	(4-serving size) JELL-O Gelatin Dessert, any 5 different flavors	**5 pkg**
6¼ cups	boiling water	**1.55 L**
1 cup	sour cream, plain yogurt, or vanilla ice cream	**250 mL**

- **DISSOLVE** 1 pkg Gelatin Dessert in 1¼ cups (300 mL) of the boiling water.
- **POUR** ¾ cup (175 mL) of the gelatin into 8 cup (2 L) ring mold. Chill until set but not firm, about 15 minutes.
- **CHILL** remaining gelatin in bowl until slightly thickened; gradually blend in 3 Tbsp (45 mL) of the sour cream. Spoon over gelatin in mold. Chill until set but not firm, about 20 to 25 minutes.
- **REPEAT** with remaining gelatin flavors.
- **CHILL** until firm, about 4 hours or overnight.
- **TO UNMOLD,** dip mold in warm water for about 10 seconds. Gently pull gelatin from around edges with moist fingers. Place moistened serving plate on top of mold. Invert mold and plate; holding mold and plate together, shake slightly to loosen. Gently remove mold and center gelatin on plate.

MAKES 12 servings.

TIP: *Use a wire whisk to add sour cream for a smoother gelatin mixture.*

Above: Rainbow Ribbon Dessert

Peach Melba Dessert

Prep time: 1½ hours   Chill time: 4 hours or overnight

1 pkg	(4-serving size) JELL-O Raspberry Gelatin Dessert	**1 pkg**
2 cups	boiling water, divided	**500 mL**
1½ cups	vanilla ice cream, softened	**375 mL**
1 pkg	(4-serving size) JELL-O Peach or Lemon Gelatin Dessert	**1 pkg**
¾ cup	cold water	**175 mL**
1 can	(14 oz/398 mL) sliced peaches, drained	**1 can**
½ cup	fresh or frozen, thawed, raspberries	**125 mL**

▼ **DISSOLVE** raspberry Gelatin Dessert in 1 cup (250 mL) boiling water. Add ice cream by spoonfuls and whisk until melted and smooth. Pour into 6 cup (1.5 L) glass serving bowl. Chill until set but not firm, about 2 hours.

▼ **MEANWHILE** dissolve peach Gelatin Dessert in remaining 1 cup (250 mL) boiling water. Add cold water. Chill until slightly thickened, about 1¼ hours.

▼ **ARRANGE** peach slices and raspberries on ice cream layer in bowl. Gently spoon peach gelatin over fruit. Chill until firm, about 4 hours or overnight.

MAKES 10 servings.

TIP: *Peach gelatin should be of egg white consistency before spooning over fruit - add slowly. This will ensure fruit does not float.*

Above: Peach Melba Dessert

Above: Strawberry Romanoff Dessert, Melon Bubble

MELON BUBBLE

Prep time: 10 minutes   Chill time: 30 minutes

1 pkg	(4-serving size) JELL-O Strawberry-Kiwi or Lemon Gelatin Dessert	**1 pkg**
1 cup	boiling water	**250 mL**
2 cups	ice cubes	**500 mL**
1 cup	melon balls	**250 mL**

- ▼ **PREPARE** Gelatin Dessert according to 30 Minute Set Method on package. Set aside ⅔ cup (150 mL) of slightly thickened gelatin.
- ▼ **STIR** melon balls into remaining gelatin; spoon into dessert dishes.
- ▼ **BEAT** reserved gelatin with electric mixer until fluffy and doubled in volume. Spoon over first fruited layer.
- ▼ **CHILL** until set, 30 minutes.

MAKES 4 servings.

TIP: *For best results when beating gelatin, place in a 4 cup (1 L) pyrex measuring cup and beat on high speed.*

STRAWBERRY ROMANOFF DESSERT

Prep time: 30 minutes   Chill time: 4 hours or overnight

2 pkg	(4-serving size) JELL-O Strawberry Gelatin Dessert	**2 pkg**
2 cups	boiling water	**500 mL**
3 Tbsp	orange liqueur or orange juice	**45 mL**
½ cup	cold water	**125 mL**
2 cups	thawed COOL WHIP Whipped Topping	**500 mL**
10 oz	frozen unsweetened strawberries, thawed (do not drain)	**300 g**

- ▼ **DISSOLVE** Gelatin Desserts in boiling water. Measure 1¼ cups (300 mL) gelatin; add undrained strawberries. Into remaining gelatin add liqueur and cold water. Chill until slightly thickened, about 1¼ hours.
- ▼ **FOLD** topping into chilled gelatin. Pour into a 6 cup (1.5 L) glass serving bowl. Carefully spoon reserved gelatin mixture over layer in bowl. Chill until firm, about 4 hours or overnight.

MAKES 8 servings.

TIP: *For Raspberry Romanoff, substitute JELL-O Raspberry Gelatin Dessert and frozen whole raspberries. Recipe may be doubled.*

Above: Lemon Charlotte With Raspberry Sauce

LEMON CHARLOTTE WITH RASPBERRY SAUCE

Prep time: 40 minutes   Chill time: 4 hours or overnight

Lemon Charlotte

1½ pkg	(3 oz/85 g **each**) lady fingers*	**1½ pkg**
1 pkg	(4-serving size) JELL-O Lemon Pudding & Pie Filling	**1 pkg**
8 oz	PHILADELPHIA Cream Cheese, softened	**250 g**
1 envelope	(7 g) unflavored gelatin	**1 envelope**
2 Tbsp	lemon juice	**25 mL**
1 tsp	grated lemon rind	**5 mL**
2 cups	thawed COOL WHIP Whipped Topping	**500 mL**

**Or use 2 pkg (7 oz/200 g each) Raspberry Swiss Rolls, sliced*

Raspberry Sauce

10 oz	frozen unsweetened raspberries, thawed	**300 g**
⅓ cup	granulated sugar	**75 mL**

LEMON CHARLOTTE:

▼ **ARRANGE** lady fingers on sides and bottom of 9 inch (23 cm) springform pan. (Refer to page 115 for tips on lady fingers.) (If desired, brush lady fingers with Sherry before placing in pan.)

▼ **PREPARE** lemon pudding and pie filling mix as directed on package, reserving the egg whites. Beat cream cheese until light and fluffy. Add warm pie filling; mix well.

▼ **SPRINKLE** gelatin over lemon juice; let stand 5 minutes. Stir into hot pie filling with lemon rind. Cover surface of mixture with plastic wrap; chill to cool down but not set, about 30 minutes.

▼ **BEAT** egg whites until stiff peaks form; fold into topping. Gently whisk lemon mixture until smooth. Fold into topping mixture. Spoon mixture into prepared pan.

▼ **CHILL** at least 4 hours or overnight. If desired garnish with slivers of candied lemon peel. Serve with raspberry sauce.

MAKES 10 to 12 servings.

RASPBERRY SAUCE:

▼ **COMBINE** raspberries and sugar. Heat over medium heat until boiling. Remove. Sieve to remove seeds, if desired. Chill.

TIP: *To make Candied Peel - Remove peel from one lemon. Cut into thin strips. Cover rind with cold water. Bring to a boil; drain water. Repeat process 3 times. Combine ½ cup (125 mL) water and ¼ cup (50 mL) sugar in saucepan. Bring to a boil. Add lemon strips. Simmer until strips are translucent. Remove from syrup and place on waxed paper. Decorate top of cake with peel.*

FRUIT FLAN DELUXE

Prep time: 30 minutes   Baking time: 12 minutes   Chill time: 3 hours

1 cup	all-purpose flour	**250 mL**
2 Tbsp	powdered sugar	**25 mL**
½ cup	butter	**125 mL**
1 pkg	(6-serving size) JELL-O Vanilla Pudding & Pie Filling	**1 pkg**
2½ cups	milk	**625 mL**
	Any selection of canned or fresh fruit (i.e. strawberries, peaches, apricots, pears, grapes, mandarin oranges, blueberries)	
½ cup	Apricot Jam	**125 mL**
1 Tbsp	lemon juice	**15 mL**
1 Tbsp	orange liqueur or orange juice	**15 mL**

- **SIFT** flour and powdered sugar together in mixing bowl. Cut in butter until mixture resembles coarse meal. Form into a ball. Chill 30 minutes. Press firmly onto bottom and sides of a 9 inch (23 cm) flan pan or pie plate. Bake at 425°F (220°C) for 10 to 12 minutes until golden brown. Cool in pan.
- **PREPARE** pudding with the milk as directed on package. Place plastic wrap on surface of pudding; chill 30 minutes.
- **WHISK** chilled pudding until smooth. Pour into flan shell.
- **ARRANGE** fruits attractively to cover surface of pudding.
- **HEAT** apricot jam, lemon juice and liqueur over low heat until melted. Remove from heat and sieve. Cool slightly and spoon over fruit.
- **CHILL** until set, 3 hours. Remove from flan pan and serve.

MAKES 8 servings.

TIP: *For easy mixing, the pastry may be made in a food processor.*

Above: Fruit Flan Deluxe

LIGHT'N FRUITY RASPBERRY PIE

Prep time: 20 minutes   Chill time: 3 hours

1 pkg	(4-serving size) JELL-O Raspberry Gelatin Dessert	**1 pkg**
$^{2}/_{3}$ cup	boiling water	**150 mL**
2 cups	ice cubes	**500 mL**
4 cups	thawed COOL WHIP Whipped Topping	**1 L**
1 cup	raspberries, fresh or frozen, thawed and drained	**250 mL**
1	prepared graham cracker crumb crust (6 ounces)	**1**

▼ **DISSOLVE** Gelatin Dessert in boiling water. Add ice cubes and stir constantly until gelatin starts to thicken, 3 to 5 minutes. Remove any unmelted ice.

▼ **WHISK** in whipped topping gently until smooth. Fold in fruit. Chill until slightly thickened, about 15 minutes.

▼ **SPOON** into crust. Chill 3 hours.

MAKES 8 servings.

TIP: *A wire whisk works well to blend gelatin and whipped topping.*

Above: Light'n Fruity Raspberry Pie

LAYERED PINEAPPLE SALAD

Prep time: 15 minutes Chilling time: 4 hours or overnight

1 pkg	(4-serving size) JELL-O Lemon Gelatin Dessert	**1 pkg**
4 cups	boiling water, divided	**1 L**
1 cup	miniature marshmallows	**250 mL**
8 oz	PHILADELPHIA Cream Cheese, softened	**250 g**
2 cups	thawed COOL WHIP Whipped Topping	**500 mL**
1 can	(14 oz/398 mL) crushed pineapple, drained	**1 can**
½ cup	chopped walnuts	**125 mL**
2 pkg	(4-serving size) JELL-O Strawberry Gelatin Dessert	**2 pkg**

▼ **DISSOLVE** lemon Gelatin Dessert in 1 cup (250 mL) boiling water; cool slightly. Add marshmallows and cream cheese. Beat with an electric mixer on low speed until smooth; chill until slightly thickened.

▼ **STIR** whipped topping, pineapple and walnuts into partially set gelatin. Pour into a 2 qt (2 L) deep bowl. Chill until set but not firm, about 1 hour.

▼ **DISSOLVE** strawberry Gelatin Dessert in remaining 3 cups (750 mL) boiling water; cool.

▼ **POUR** cooled gelatin over lemon cream cheese mixture and chill until set, about 4 hours or overnight.

MAKES 10 to 12 servings.

TIP: *A great party recipe. Eliminate walnuts, if desired.*

Above: Layered Pineapple Salad

INDEX